CREATION

of the

MODERN MIDDLE EAST

Jordan

CREATION

of the

MODERN MIDDLE EAST

Iran, Second Edition

Iraq, Second Edition

Israel, Second Edition

Jordan, Second Edition

Lebanon

The Palestinian National Authority,
Second Edition

Saudi Arabia, Second Edition

Syria, Second Edition

Turkey, Second Edition

United Arab Emirates

CREATION

of the

MODERN MIDDLE EAST

Jordan

Second Edition

Hal Marcovitz | Series Editor: Arthur Goldschmidt Jr.

CHELSEA HOUSE
PUBLISHERS

An imprint of Infobase Publishing

Jordan, Second Edition

Copyright © 2009 by Infobase Publishing

Chelsea House
An imprint of Infobase Publishing
132 West 31st Street
New York NY 10001

Library of Congress Cataloging-in-Publication Data
Marcovitz, Hal.
 Jordan / by Hal Marcovitz. — 2nd ed.
   p. cm. — (Creation of the modern Middle East)
 Includes bibliographical references and index.
 ISBN 978-1-60413-018-8 (hardcover)
 1. Jordan—History—1946-1952—Juvenile literature. 2. Jordan—History—1952-1999—Juvenile literature. 3. Jordan--History—1999—Juvenile literature. I. Title. II. Series.
 DS154.53.M37 2008
 956.9504'3—dc22   2008016978

Series design by Annie O'Donnell
Cover design by Jooyoung An

Printed in the United States of America

Bang EJB 10 9 8 7 6 5 4 3 2 1

This book is printed on acid-free paper.

Contents

Jordan's 9–11

As war raged in Iraq, the people of Jordan watched the volatile situation in the country on their eastern border with a growing sense of fear. They had good reason. Each day, thousands of Iraqi refugees streamed into Jordan. With the Iraqi insurgency growing bolder by the day, the Jordanians feared that the insurgents planned to spread their violent brand of Islamic fundamentalism elsewhere in the region—particularly into Jordan. They suspected that many terrorists were entering their country in the guise of refugees.

In fact, violence had come to be a way of life in many Middle East countries—particularly after the U.S. invasion of Iraq in 2003. The war helped fuel the anger of Islamic fundamentalists who oppose Western influences they believe run counter to the teachings of Muhammad, the seventh-century prophet who founded the Islamic faith.

For years, the government of Jordan had infuriated Islamic extremists because of its strong support of the United States. That policy was followed by Jordan's longtime king, Hussein ibn Talal, who also signed a treaty with Israel, Jordan's western neighbor and another target of Islamic extremism. When King Hussein died in 1999, his son and successor, Abdullah II, continued his country's strong support for the United States and Israel.

Jordanians had already seen acts of terrorism committed in their country. In 2002, Laurence Foley, a U.S. diplomat stationed in Jordan, had been murdered by terrorists in the front yard of his home in Amman, the Jordanian capital. Two men were arrested, convicted, and sentenced to death in the Foley

Abu Musab al-Zarqawi in 2002 *(left)* and in 2004 *(right)*. A native Jordanian, al-Zarqawi was originally in charge of a small insurgency in Iraq, but later allied himself with al-Qaeda. As leader of the Iraqi branch of this terrorist organization, al-Zarqawi ordered violent attacks against foreign-owned businesses and the Jordanian public.

murder. Another six men were connected to the plot, including the brutally violent head of the terrorist organization al-Qaeda in Iraq, Abu Musab al-Zarqawi, a Jordanian and leader of the Iraqi insurgency.

Following the Foley murder, al-Zarqawi promised more violence in Jordan. He released a secretly recorded videotape in which he said, "As the days go by, we will have more fierce confrontations with the Jordanian government. The chapters of some of these confrontations have ended, but what is coming is more vicious and bitter."

In August 2005, al-Zarqawi's organization struck again. That month, an al-Qaeda terror cell in Iraq smuggled three Russian-made rockets into Jordan—the cell members brought the rockets over the border by hiding them in the gas tank of a car. The rockets were fired at two U.S. Navy warships anchored near the Jordanian port city of Aqaba. The rockets missed their targets—they struck land, killing a Jordanian soldier. Despite missing the ships, al-Zarqawi promised more attacks in Jordan. Four months after the Aqaba attack, he would keep his promise.

TERROR STRIKES AMMAN

In the 1920s, Amman was little more than a dusty desert crossroads where Bedouin traders made camp to water their camels. By the dawn of the twenty-first century, Amman had grown into a bustling metropolis of more than 2 million people. Jordan's capital is widely recognized as one of the leading commercial and banking centers of the Middle East. Hussein and later Abdullah had encouraged investment by Western corporations and financiers, which were drawn to Amman because of Jordan's stability and its reputation for peaceful coexistence with its neighbors. "Jordan has come out ahead because we alone among the nations in this region have been able to use our safety and stability as our major selling points," said Adnan Abu Odeh, a former Jordanian ambassador to the United Nations.

Among the Western corporations that had elected to invest in Amman were some of America's largest hotel chains. In downtown Amman, three of the most familiar buildings are the

Mediterranean Sea

LEBANON

Golan
Heights

Sea of
Galilee

Yarmuk R.

SYRIA

IRAQ

SYRIAN

Mahattat al-Jufur

DESERT

Irbid

Jarash

Al Mafraq

West
Bank

Salt

Jordan R.

Az Zarqa

Mahattat al-Hafif

Amman

Azraq ash Shishan

Dead Sea

Ma'daba

JORDAN

Al Mazra'ah

ISRAEL

Al Karak

AS SAWWAN PLAIN

SAUDI ARABIA

At Tafilah

Ba'ir

Ash Shawbak

Ma'an

AL JAFR
DEPRESSION

Ra's an Naqb

Mt. Ramm
▲ 5,689 ft.

N

Aqaba

Gulf of
Aqaba

© Infobase Publishing

| 0 | 50 miles |
| 0 | 50 km |

Israeli-occupied with current
status subject to the Israeli-
Palestinian Interim Agreement.
Permanent status to be
determined through further
negotiation.

Israeli-occupied area

Slightly smaller than Indiana, Jordan shares the longest border with Israel and is
surrounded by Syria, Iraq, and Saudi Arabia. Almost entirely landlocked, it has a
Mediterranean climate with cool winters and hot dry summers. The country has
limited access to freshwater, and less than five percent of its territory is suitable for
agriculture.

Grand Hyatt Hotel, Radisson SAS Hotel, and the Days Inn. All three hotels are used not only by visiting executives, journalists, military leaders, and diplomats but also by Jordanians who rent the huge ballrooms of the hotels to stage weddings and other gala events.

In fact, on the evening of November 9, 2005, a wedding reception was in progress in the Philadelphia Ballroom of the Radisson, where Jordanians Ashraf Daas and his new wife, Nadia Alami, were celebrating their wedding along with some 200 guests. Unknown to the newlyweds or their families and friends, two unwanted guests had blended into the jumble of people in the ballroom. They were Ali Hussein Ali al-Shamari and his wife, Sajida Mubarak Atrous al-Rishawi. Both were Iraqis who crossed into Jordan just four days before using fake passports. As they made their way through the ballroom, the couple concealed belts laden with explosives under their clothes.

Shamari and Rishawi entered the Radisson and stood at opposite ends of the Philadelphia Ballroom. Their plan was to detonate their belts simultaneously, taking their own lives as well as the lives of the hapless wedding guests who stood nearby. Their plan for the attack—a suicide bombing—had become a common technique among Muslim extremists. Suicide bombers believe that by taking their own lives they become martyrs in the cause for preserving Islam, and that they will be rewarded for their martyrdom in heaven.

At a few minutes before 9:00 P.M., Shamari jumped onto a table and detonated his belt. His wife tried to detonate her belt as well but it malfunctioned. Instead, Rishawi fell into the crowd of terrified wedding guests who scrambled to escape from the ballroom.

Just as the guests from the Radisson wedding were pouring onto the streets of Amman, two other blasts shook the city. Nearly simultaneous explosions struck the Grand Hyatt and the

After a coordinated series of bombings at three hotels in Amman on November 9, 2005, the police quickly organized an investigation to collect evidence *(above)* and find the culprits. These attacks killed 60 people and injured 115 others. Al-Qaeda claimed responsibility, linking the blasts against foreign-owned businesses and the Jordanian public to the U.S. invasion of Iraq.

Days Inn. "I never expected something like this to happen in Jordan," said Marwan Qusos, a nightclub owner who lost two friends in the Grand Hyatt blast.

The death toll from the three blasts totaled 60 with another 115 injured. Thirty-eight of the casualties were guests at the wedding of Ashraf Daas and Nadia Alami. The bride and groom both survived the blast but Ashraf lost his father and 16 of his father's relatives while Nadia lost her father, mother, and nine other family members. Ashraf's younger brother, Bashar Daas, said the terrorists had turned what should have been the most joyful event in the lives of the newlyweds into what will clearly be the saddest day in their lives. "We were waiting for this day since they met three years ago," said Bashar. "He knew at the start he would marry her. The best day became the worst."

Also among the dead were three Chinese military officers and four Americans, including Moustapha Akkad, a Syrian-American and Hollywood film executive who produced the *Halloween* series of horror films. Most of the other victims were Jordanians.

The United States suffered a much more severe terrorist attack on September 11, 2001, when airliners hijacked by Muslim extremists crashed into the World Trade Center in New York City and the Pentagon near Washington, D.C., taking the lives of more than 3,000 people. The September 11 attacks led to the U.S. invasion of Iraq, a country that American political leaders accused of providing aid to the terrorists. That charge eventually proved to be without substance; nevertheless, the government of Iraqi dictator Saddam Hussein was regarded as one of the most repressive and tyrannical in the world. In late 2006, Hussein was executed by the new Iraqi government.

In the United States, the September 11 attacks has become known by the abbreviation 9–11, because it is common for Americans to shorten dates by placing the month before the day. Elsewhere in the world, including Jordan, people abbreviate the dates by placing the day before the month. Therefore, the three hotel attacks of November 9, 2005, have become known as Jordan's 9–11.

RISHAWI ARRESTED

Hours after the three hotel blasts, King Abdullah appeared on Jordanian television to assure his citizens that the terrorists responsible for the hotel bombings would be brought to justice.

"We will pursue these criminals and those who are behind them, and we will reach them wherever they are," Abdullah said. "We will pull them from their holes and bring them to justice."

Within days of the blasts, Jordanian police tracked down and arrested Sajida al-Rishawi, whom they discovered is the sister of a high-ranking leader of al-Qaeda in Iraq. Rishawi told police that her husband planned the attacks, and that the couple entered the country with the two other conspirators, who set off the charges at the Grand Hyatt and the Days Inn. A few days after her arrest, Rishawi told her story on national television in Jordan. She said:

> My husband wore one [bomb] belt and I another—he told me how to use it. . . . We went into the hotel. He [my husband] took one corner and I another. There was a wedding in the hotel. There were women and children. My husband executed the attack. I tried to detonate and failed. I left. People started running and I started running with them.

Jordan is not the only country that has suffered terrorist attacks for its support of the United States. In 2004, bombs exploded at a train station in Madrid, Spain, killing 191 people. A year later, on July 7, three subway trains and a bus in London, England, were attacked by suicide bombers, who took the lives of 52 people and injured 700. Both countries have served as U.S. allies in Iraq. Following the Madrid attack, the Spanish government announced plans to withdraw its token force of 1,300 troops from Iraq. Great Britain has remained a staunch U.S. ally. Following the London transit attacks, also known as the 7-7 bombings, the country maintained a significant fighting force in Iraq through 2007, when the British army, after stabilizing portions of the country under its control, started drawing down its troops.

Although Jordan has played no combat role in Iraq, King Abdullah did not back down from his country's commitment to support the U.S. mission in Iraq. Amman has continued to serve as a headquarters for many of the private contractors who are rebuilding the Iraqi infrastructure destroyed by the war. Also, many U.S. combat units heading for Iraq have been allowed to remain temporarily on Jordanian soil as they prepare to assume responsibilities in the war zone.

In the days following the Amman hotel blasts, many Jordanians attended rallies in support of their country and to denounce violence—much as many Americans came together shortly after the World Trade Center and the Pentagon attacks. Many people fixed Jordanian flags to the antennas of their cars, similar to how many Americans showed their patriotism following the September 11 attacks. Said King Abdullah, "I know very well the courage of the Jordanians, and their response to these events had exceeded all expectations. Jordanians are fearless, and terrorism will not affect their morale or their determination."

THE END OF AL-ZARQAWI

Abu Musab al-Zarqawi's reign of terror ended just seven months later. A year before the Amman hotel bombings, al-Zarqawi murdered Nicholas Berg, an American civilian captured in the Iraqi capital of Baghdad and broadcast it over the Internet. Following the Berg murder, U.S. armed forces in Iraq stepped up their search for the terrorist. On June 7, 2006, U.S. intelligence officials tracked al-Zarqawi to an isolated house just a few miles north of Baqubah. Two U.S. Air Force planes were dispatched; they unleashed missiles at the house, leveling the structure and killing the occupants. When ground troops arrived to sift through the rubble, they found al-Zarqawi barely alive. He died minutes later.

As for Sajida al-Rishawi, the Iraqi woman was tried for the murders of the victims of the Amman hotel bombings in 2006. She insisted at her trial that she is innocent and was duped into wearing the bomb-laden belt by her husband. The Jordanian military court refused to believe her story. She was convicted and sentenced to death by hanging.

Revolt Against the Turks

Soon after the end of World War I, the British government was faced with the rather thorny job of fulfilling conflicting promises it had made to Jews and Arabs, two groups of people who were longtime rivals for the possession of Palestine, a territory sacred to both.

In 1917, the British government had adopted the Balfour Declaration, issued by foreign secretary Arthur James Balfour, supporting the desire of Jews to establish a nation in Palestine—land claimed by the Jews since the time of the Hebrew kings in the tenth century. By 1917, the British army was already occupying Palestine, having seized the territory during World War I from the Turks, who had ruled the region for centuries. In 1922, the League of Nations—a forerunner of the United Nations (UN)—adopted the British Mandate, giving the British authority over Palestine until they deemed the Palestinians ready to govern themselves. The League of Nations incorporated the Balfour Declaration into the mandate, meaning the British were to pursue the creation of a Jewish homeland. When the war ended in 1918, the Jews of Palestine expected Great Britain to support their independence.

While the British made promises to the Jews, they also made promises to the Arabs. In 1916, prompted by the British, Arab leaders staged the Great Arab Revolt against the Ottoman Empire, who were part of the Central Powers (Germany, Austria-Hungary, and Bulgaria). For four centuries, the Arabs had been ruled by the Ottoman Turks. As fellow Muslims, they acquiesced to Turkish rule for most of that time, but by the twentieth century, Ottoman Turkish power and influence were waning. Now referred to as the "Sick Man of Europe," the Ottoman Empire was corrupt, inefficient, and increasingly resented by many Arabs. The Ottoman sultan could no longer depend on the loyalty of his troops. Their officers, the so-called "Young Turks" rebelled in 1908 to bring constitutional rule to the empire. Many Arabs initially supported the Young Turks but turned against them when these new rulers proved just as oppressive as the sultans had ever been. Arab leader Sharif Hussein—the *sharif* is leader of the Prophet Muhammad's descendents—reached an agreement with the British during the war to rebel against Ottoman rule. The Arabs fought bravely on the side of the British, advised by one of their officers, T.E. Lawrence, who supported the Arabs' right to independence and taught them some techniques of guerrilla warfare.

Once the war was over, the British found themselves facing not only the demands of the Arabs and the Jews, but their own self-interests as well. Even in the early years of the twentieth century, the Middle East was recognized as a source of tremendous oil reserves. As industry in Western nations began relying more and more on the gasoline-fueled internal combustion engine, political leaders realized a guaranteed source of oil would be vital to their countries' economies. Great Britain, which also desired a guaranteed source of oil for its navy, aimed to control those oil reserves. So did France, which emerged from the war with its industries shattered and its people destitute but, nevertheless, on the winning side.

The strategic importance of the Middle East to Great Britain as well as to other world powers also went beyond oil interests. Armies stationed in Turkey and Iran could be dispatched to Russia, if necessary, to intervene in the civil war that was raging in that country.

The land at the hub of this valuable region was territory in western Arabia that was rocky, untillable, and mountainous; it

T.E. Lawrence *(above)* was sent by the British to help organize the Middle Eastern forces in a revolt against the Turks (1916–1918). Lawrence, an experienced archaeologist who spoke Arabic, joined the local rebels and employed guerrilla tactics that destroyed what was left of the Ottoman Empire.

was a land separating the two great Middle East capitals of Cairo and Damascus, occupied mostly by nomadic Bedouin tribesmen because no one else wanted to live there. On a map, this land could be found along the east bank of the Jordan River.

THE FIRST SETTLEMENTS

The first settlements in this region were established along the Jordan River some 5,000 years ago. The Shasu, early nomadic tribesmen, were among the first settlers. By 1500 B.C., the land was part of Canaan, the territory conquered by the Egyptians that now includes Israel, Jordan, and Syria. According to the Bible, it was at about this time that the Jews were freed from bondage in Egypt by Moses and wandered in the desert for 40 years before finding their homeland across the Jordan River. Just before crossing the river, they stopped so Moses could ascend Mount Nebo in Jordan, where he died. The Israelite leader Joshua then led the Jews across the river to Palestine. The Jews built a kingdom across the river, where they were led by the kings Saul, David, and Solomon.

During the next several centuries, the land was ruled by a series of conquering peoples—the Assyrians, Babylonians, Persians, Greeks, and Romans among them. In the early fourth century A.D., the emperor Constantine, who had made Christianity the state religion of the Roman Empire, conquered what is now Jordan and, during the next three centuries, most of the people in this region became Christian. In A.D. 610 a merchant in Mecca, Muhammad, began to hear voices that he believed came from God, and soon the Arab world would be changed forever.

Known as the Prophet, Muhammad at first led a normal and quite unremarkable life in the Arabian city of Mecca. He was born into the Hashem clan about A.D. 570. He married at 25, taking for his wife Khadija, a rich widow 15 years his senior.

When he was 40, Muhammad began to hear and see supernatural beings. One of these took the form of the angel Gabriel, who told Muhammad: "Recite thou, in the name of thy Lord who created; created man from clots of blood. Recite thou, for thy Lord is the most beneficient, who has taught the use of the pen; hath taught man that which he knoweth not."

God, or Allah in Arabic, then commanded Muhammad to repeat his words, which came to be known as the Qur'an—the set of beliefs revealed to Muhammad by the angel Gabriel. It took several years for Muhammad to recite the beliefs. His words were recorded on scraps of leather, flat stone tablets, even camel bones.

In English, *Islam* means "submission to God." Believers in this religion accept its five pillars: *shahada*—the tenet that there is one god, Allah, and one messenger, Muhammad; *salat*—the duty to pray five times a day; *sawn*—the observance of Ramadan, the holy month in which Muslims refrain from eating, drinking, smoking, and sex from dawn to sundown; *zakat*—the duty of donating a share of one's income or property to the needy; and, finally, making at least one pilgrimage, or *hajj*, in one's lifetime to the holy city of Mecca (as long as one possesses the health and financial means to make the journey).

At first, Arabs in Mecca and elsewhere refused to accept the new religion. Many of them worshiped multiple deities and rejected the idea of one supreme being. Slowly, though, the Arab people began converting. A critical event was the *hijra*, or emigration of Muhammad and his early followers from Mecca to Medina in 622. Brought to Medina to mediate a quarrel among the pagan Arab tribes living there, Muhammad created the *ummah*, or Muslim community, in these new surroundings. Some Arabs in Medina were won over by Muhammad's leadership; others by the opportunity to raid the caravans of the pagan merchants of Mecca. Eventually the Muslims subdued Mecca and won other Arabian tribesmen to their new faith.

Most of the early followers were drawn to Islam by the personal appeal of Muhammad, an enormously persuasive and charismatic leader who seemed to possess a gift for resolving disputes. Others joined Islam after they were conquered by Muslim armies. Unlike the first Christians, the Muslims were prepared to fight to spread the word of the Prophet.

In 632, having subdued most of the Arabian Peninsula, Muhammad died. His followers chose Abu Bakr to succeed him, and Abu Bakr was given the title of caliph (in Arabic, *khalifa* means "successor"). Under Abu Bakr, the Muslims began to conquer some of the lands to their north, including part of what is now Jordan. The next caliph, Umar, who reigned from 634 to 644, was a strong leader under whom the Muslims conquered lands from Persia in the east to Egypt in the west. Soon afterward, though, the Muslim people fell victim to the jealousy, ambition, and internal wrangling that would haunt their leaders throughout history, even into the twenty-first century. Umar was killed by a Persian Christian slave, and the third caliph, Uthman, was murdered by a group of Muslim rebels who favored Muhammad's cousin Ali, who became the fourth caliph. The first civil war in Islam ensued, ending in 661 with the accession of Mu'awiya, who moved the capital of the ummah to Damascus and created the Umayyad dynasty to rule over the Muslim world.

Despite these dissensions, Islam continued to expand. The great Middle Eastern cities of Damascus, Alexandria, Beirut, Jerusalem, Baghdad, and Cairo became important trading centers.

In the eleventh century, the pope and some of the Christian kings of western Europe sent soldiers of the cross, or Crusaders, to regain Jerusalem for Christianity. For about a century, there was a Christian kingdom in the lands roughly comparable to what is now Israel, occasionally including parts of what are now Jordan, Lebanon, and Syria. This kingdom was defeated in 1187 by Saladin, a great Kurdish warrior who created a Muslim empire that stretched from Egypt to Syria and Yemen.

In spite of the enmity between the Crusaders and some Muslim states, many Arab merchants and seamen traded with the Europeans. In addition, the silk route to China extended across what are now Turkey and Iran through Central Asia. The thirteenth-century Mongol conquests destroyed cities such as Baghdad but actually facilitated Europe's access to the Far East, leading to Marco Polo's famous voyages to China. The Mongols also introduced many Turkish tribes into the Middle East. One of these became a band of warriors who built up the Ottoman Empire between the fourteenth and sixteenth centuries, conquering southeastern Europe and parts of Asia. In 1516, they conquered, as a part of their push into the Arab world, what has now become Jordan. The Ottoman sultans became the rulers of North Africa, Egypt, and southwestern Asia. One of their new provinces was the Hejaz, the western part of the Arabian Peninsula that includes the Muslim holy cities of Mecca and Medina. In 1908, Ottoman sultan Abdul Hamid recognized Hussein bin Ali as the sharif of Mecca, which meant that he became the leader of the Prophet's descendents in the city to which Muslims make their *hajj*, or pilgrimage.

Born in 1853 in the Turkish capital of Constantinople (which is now known as Istanbul), Sharif Hussein was the son of an Arab father and a Circassian mother. Circassians are non-Arab Muslims from the Caucasus region of Russia just east of Turkey. Hussein was a Hashemite, a member of the Prophet Muhammad's family, and hence revered by Muslims.

But, of course, with the Turks holding sway over the Arab world, Sharif Hussein could merely oversee the rocky strip of land of the Hejaz, and even there his authority was limited. Still, Hussein knew the power of the Turks was waning.

Sharif Hussein had four sons: Faisal, Abdullah, Zeid, and Ali. The boys were educated in the cosmopolitan city of Constantinople. When they returned to the Hejaz, Hussein sent them into the desert to learn the Arab ways. "Soon they hardened and became self-reliant," wrote T.E. Lawrence, the British military officer who advised Hussein.

Of the four boys, Abdullah impressed Lawrence the most, and, indeed, Abdullah would prove himself to be a strong ruler in the years ahead. Lawrence wrote:

I began to suspect him of constant cheerfulness. His eyes had a confirmed twinkle; and though only thirty-five, he was putting on flesh. It might be due to too much laughter. Life seemed very merry for Abdulla[h]. He was short, strong, fair-skinned, with a carefully trimmed brown beard, masking his round smooth face and short lips. In manner he was open, or affected openness, and [he] was charming on acquaintance. He stood not on ceremony, but jested with all comers in most easy fashion; yet, when we fell into serious talk, the veil of humo[u]r seemed to fade away. He then chose his words, and argued shrewdly.

When World War I broke out in 1914, the Ottoman Empire sided with Germany and declared a *jihad*, or Muslim holy war, against the Allies. The British government sought a Middle Eastern ally that could win back the support of its numerous Muslim subjects in India and other parts of the British Empire. Its high commissioner in Cairo wrote to Sharif Hussein and offered him independence for the Arabs if he would lead them in a rebellion against the Turks. Hussein agreed, and the Great Arab Revolt commenced in June 1916.

Lawrence was dispatched as a military adviser to Sharif Hussein and his sons. "I vowed to make the Arab Revolt the engine of its own success as well as handmaid to [the British army's] Egyptian campaign, and vowed to lead it so madly in the final victory that expediency should counsel to the Powers a fair settlement of the Arabs' moral claims," Lawrence wrote.

The Arabs fought hard. Their biggest victories came in 1918, when Arab fighters under Hussein's son Faisal drove the Turks out of Damascus. Meanwhile, in 1917, the British government issued the Balfour Declaration, promising a Jewish national home in Palestine. Once the Arabs learned about it, they objected strongly, for they constituted the majority of Palestine's population and assumed that it had been promised to them. Actually, the British turned out to be far more duplicitous than even the Arabs suspected. Unknown to the Arabs, the British had signed the Sykes-Picot Agreement with France, essentially dividing the former Ottoman-held territories between the two powers at the conclusion of the war. Great Britain took Iraq and

After the Ottoman Empire sided with the Central Powers during World War I, the British government appealed to Sharif Hussein ibn Ali *(above)*, the ruler of the Hejaz, to become their ally, with promises of support for an independent Arab nation. Sharif Hussein and his sons led the Arab Revolt (1916–1918) but the British reneged on their promise and divided the Ottoman lands into a system of mandates and protectorates.

Palestine as well as the territory on the west bank of the Jordan River; France took Lebanon. Syria was split between the two countries—France took the capital of Damascus and most of the northern territory while Great Britain kept the land along the east bank of the Jordan. That was territory Great Britain felt it needed to serve as a buffer between Palestine and Syria. Evidently, the British did not trust the French and feared invasion of Palestine from northern Syria.

Clearly, the British had sold out the Arabs. The war ended in 1918. The Ottoman Empire was defeated. Great Britain and France as well as the Arabs and Jews all believed they had claims to the former Ottoman territories. In 1921, a British diplomat named Winston Churchill arrived in Cairo to sort out the mess.

3

Creation of Transjordan

W inston Churchill was Great Britain's colonial secretary, charged with maintaining his country's far-flung territories. He arrived in the Middle East to find a decidedly hostile group of Arabs and their leaders. He was met by Lawrence, whom Churchill enlisted as an adviser. On a tour of the region, Churchill and Lawrence stopped in Gaza in Palestine where they witnessed a riot staged by anti-Jewish demonstrators.

"I say, Lawrence—are these people dangerous?" Churchill asked. "They don't seem to be too pleased to see us. What are they shouting?"

Lawrence interpreted the words for his colonial secretary: "'Down with the British and down with Jewish policy!'"

Meanwhile, since the end of World War I, the Hashemites had laid claim to the various Arab states. An Arab congress meeting in Damascus proclaimed Faisal king of Syria. Abdullah was offered the crown of Iraq while Ali ruled the Hejaz. Sharif Hussein arrived in the Arabian city of Jiddah and proclaimed himself king of Arabia. Only Abdullah's rule would endure, and it would not be in Iraq.

In 1920, France laid claim to Syria, deposing Faisal. Sharif Hussein would soon be a victim of a coup staged by Abdul Aziz ibn Saud; henceforth, the country would be known as Saudi Arabia. The Saudis would eventually swallow up the Hejaz, ending Hashemite rule there as well.

As for Abdullah, at the Cairo Conference Churchill told him that the British intended to stay in Iraq, which was rebelling at the time, and that Faisal—not Abdullah—would rule in Baghdad under their mandate. He also made it clear that the British intended to abide by the Balfour Declaration:

> You have asked me in the first place to repudiate the Balfour Declaration and to veto immigration of Jews into Palestine. . . . It is not in my power to do so, nor, if it were in my power, would it be my wish. The British [G]overnment have passed their word, by the mouth of Mr. Balfour, that they will view with favour the establishment of a National Home for Jews in Palestine, and that inevitably involves the immigration of Jews into the country. This declaration of Mr. Balfour and of the British [G]overnment has been ratified by the Allied Powers who have been victorious in the Great War; and it was a declaration made while the war was still in progress, while victory and defeat hung in the balance. It must therefore be regarded as one of the facts definitely established by the triumphant conclusion of the Great War. . . .

To compensate Abdullah, Churchill offered him authority over the lands of southern Syria along the eastern bank of the Jordan River. Churchill called it Transjordan, meaning "across Jordan." To sweeten the deal, Churchill promised a British subsidy and British army officers to arm and train the Transjordanian army—which Churchill suggested Abdullah use to protect Palestine.

Transjordan was hardly the prize Sharif Hussein or his sons had in mind when they dreamed of a vast Hashemite empire stretching from Damascus to Baghdad to Mecca. Indeed, the land Churchill offered to Abdullah covered just 34,500 square miles—roughly the size of the state of Indiana. Fewer than 10,000 people lived in the new state's territory. Amman, which would be the capital, was hardly the cosmopolitan center of trade that visitors found in Damascus or Baghdad. Moreover, the land was rocky and untillable—to this day, barely 5 percent of the country is farmed. And, finally, there were no known oil reserves in Transjordan. Nearly a century later, there are still none.

Churchill told Abdullah that he expected him to rule as a constitutional monarch, meaning the people of Transjordan would elect a parliament, although Abdullah as emir, or prince, would have final authority over affairs of state. Churchill said diplomats from Great Britain would be dispatched to Amman to advise the new government. Churchill also made it clear that Transjordan would, for the time being, remain under a British mandate—that it would exist as a state within the British Empire. There would be no immediate independence for the new state, but Churchill promised Abdullah that could come in time.

Abdullah had no choice. On March 30, 1921, he accepted Churchill's offer.

The colonial secretary returned to England, where he would eventually ascend to prime minister and face greater challenges. By creating Transjordan, Churchill was certain that he fulfilled the pledge the British government made to Sharif Hussein in 1916.

But Lawrence knew the truth. He wrote:

The Cabinet raised the Arabs to fight for us by definite promises of self-government afterward[s]. Arabs believe in persons, not in institutions. They saw in me a free agent of the British [G]overnment, and demanded from me an endorsement of its written promises. So I had to join the conspiracy, and, for what my word was worth, assured the men of their reward. In our two years' partnership under fire they grew accustomed to believing me and to think my [G]overnment, like myself, sincere. In this hope they performed some fine things, but, of course, instead of being proud of what we did together, I was continually and bitterly ashamed.

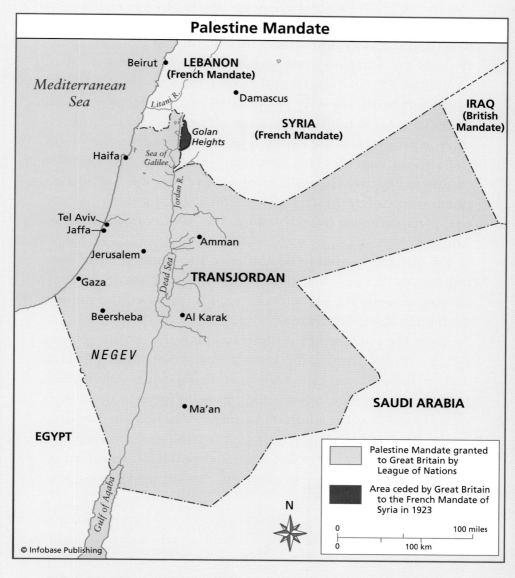

Palestine Mandate

Mediterranean
Sea

Beirut ● **LEBANON**
(French Mandate)

● Damascus

SYRIA
(French Mandate)

Litani R.

Golan
Heights

Haifa ● *Sea of Galilee*

Tel Aviv
Jaffa ●

Jerusalem ●

● Amman

Jordan R.

● Gaza

Dead Sea

TRANSJORDAN

Beersheba ●

● Al Karak

NEGEV

● Ma'an

SAUDI ARABIA

EGYPT

Gulf of Aqaba

IRAQ
(British
Mandate)

N

| | Palestine Mandate granted to Great Britain by League of Nations |
| Area ceded by Great Britain to the French Mandate of Syria in 1923 |

0   100 miles

0   100 km

© Infobase Publishing

In 1922, the British divided the Kingdom of Jordan into two parts, designating all lands west of the Jordan River as Palestine and lands east of the river as Transjordan. The precise geographical boundaries were disputed due to conflicting promises made to Jewish and Arab interests by the Balfour Declaration, the Sykes-Picot Agreement, the Hussein-McMahon Correspondence, and the Churchill White Paper.

A ROUGH BEGINNING

When Abdullah arrived in Transjordan, he found unforgiving deserts and rocky mountains. Amman, the capital of his country, was certainly no desert oasis, but it did have a railroad depot and was an important stop on a railway that connected Damascus with the city of Medina in the Hejaz. Amman traces its roots to biblical times and was named for the Ammonites, a people who are believed to have shared ancestry with the ancient Israelites. In the third century B.C., the city was conquered by the Greek ruler of Egypt, Ptolemy II Philadelphus, who called the city Philadelphia. By the third century A.D., after conquest by Arab tribes, the city became known as Amman.

Despite the hardscrabble nature of the country, there were indications that people had carved civilizations out of the Transjordan wilderness long before Churchill conceived the country during the Cairo Conference.

From the late seventh century to about the second century B.C., a nomadic Arab tribe known as the Nabataeans arrived and established the city known as Petra, where the homes, temples, tombs, and other buildings were carved out of solid rock. About 75 miles south of Amman, Petra is located so deep in the Jebel Mubak Mountains that it remained undiscovered until the nineteenth century, when archaeologists stumbled on the ruins. The only way to enter the city is through a narrow, winding gorge.

The Nabataeans were skilled engineers. They conceived of a way to channel water into their mountain city some 300 years before the Romans built their first aqueduct, the Aqua Appia, to channel fresh water into Rome. With the availability of water, Petra was able to grow into a city of some 30,000 people. "We were astonished by how sophisticated their ideas were," said Maan al-Huneidi, the Jordanian archaeologist who is heading a project to uncover parts of Petra that are still buried. Indeed, it is believed that as much as two-thirds of the ancient city lies beneath the surface. Jordanian officials remain committed to uncovering Petra, which has become one of the country's main tourist destinations.

The country is also the location of the Iraq al Amir—the "Caves of the Prince." Located about 15 miles southwest of Amman in a dry river valley known as Wadi Seer, the 11 caves are cut into the side of a mountain and are believed to have been hand carved some 6,000 years ago. And in southwest Jordan, about 45 miles south of Petra, lies Wadi Rum, a valley of sandstone and granite featuring stunning, vertical-walled cliffs. Lawrence, who rode through the valley, was awed by what he saw. He wrote:

> The ascent became gentle, till the valley was a confined tilted plain. The hills on the right grew taller and sharper, a fair counterpart of the other side which straightened itself to one massive rampart of redness. They drew together until only two miles divided them: and then, towering gradually till their parallel parapets must have been a thousand feet above us, ran forward in an avenue for miles.
>
> They were not unbroken walls of rock, but were built sectionally, in crags like gigantic buildings, along the two sides of their street. Deep alleys, fifty feet across, divided the crags, whose planes were smoothed by the weather into huge apses and bays, and enriched with surface fretting and fracture, like design. Caverns high up on the precipice were round like windows; others near the foot gaped like doors.

Other sites of historical importance in Jordan are Jerash, a city built by Roman conquerors, and Ajloun, site of a twelfth-century Arab castle named Qala'at al-Rabad, which was erected atop a 4,000-foot mountain for defense against Crusaders. Indeed, it seemed to Abdullah that a people resourceful enough to carve a city out of stone or erect a castle atop a mountain were up to the task of building Transjordan.

Petra, an ancient city once closed off to foreigners, is one of Jordan's most famous sites. As one of the New Seven Wonders of the World, the entire city is carved into the red, pink, and white cliffs that surround the area. One of their most famous structures, the Treasury Building *(above)*, was featured in the movie *Indiana Jones and the Last Crusade*.

But while there was no shortage of ancient ruins across the Transjordanian landscape, there was a definite lack of everything else. There were no hospitals and just a handful of schools. There were few paved roads, few farms, and no industry.

And there were few Transjordanians. None of the people living in Transjordan in 1921 regarded themselves as Transjordanians; they were Syrians, Arabians, or even Circassians. Almost all were nomadic Bedouins, who for centuries had been crossing what was now regarded as the Transjordanian border.

TRANSJORDAN OPENS ITS DOORS

To build his country, Abdullah welcomed help from the outside. More than any other Arab leader, he accepted Jewish settlers and invited some of their engineers to plan roads and electric power plants. He also welcomed the Palestinian Christians who discovered phosphate deposits in Transjordan. Today, this substance, which is an important ingredient of fertilizer, is the country's largest export.

Still, throughout its first decades of existence, Transjordan was a poor country. Abdullah and other members of the royal family shared in that poverty. A residence for the emir was not constructed until 1925. Until that time, Abdullah lived modestly in the homes of tribal leaders, who were honored to share their quarters with the emir. For several months each year, Abdullah lived as a Bedouin, pitching his tent in the desert near the Dead Sea after a long march atop a camel. At night, he would dine with friends in his tent. It was a lifestyle he preferred.

Other members of Abdullah's family were not as fortunate. On November 14, 1935, his grandson Hussein ibn Talal was born. Hussein was the son of Talal, the crown prince, and his wife, Princess Zein. Talal and his family lived in a modest, unheated home in Amman. Hussein's baby sister would later die of pneumonia, and Talal was beginning to show signs of deteriorating mental health.

BRITISH INTERFERENCE

Meanwhile, the British kept their promise to arm and train a Transjordanian army. General Frederick Peake was dispatched from duty in Egypt to create the army, which was known as the Arab Legion. Under Peake, the Arab Legion would become the best-trained and hardest-fighting army in the Arab states. In 1928, Peake was succeeded by Major General John Bagot Glubb, who would supervise the Arab Legion into the 1950s.

A number of British advisers served in Amman. Abdullah barely tolerated most of these advisers, finding them to be meddlers who failed to understand Arab ways and looked on Transjordan as a British colony under their authority. It seemed to Abdullah that the British government's representatives in his capital were more interested in looking after British interests than in solving his country's enormous problems.

An exception was Alec Kirkbride, a former British army major. Kirkbride and Abdullah grew very close; Kirkbride would remain in Amman as an adviser to the emir and later served as British ambassador to the country until Abdullah's death in 1951.

To administer Jordan, the British had established three regional governments, each headed by a high council composed of sheikhs who led local clans or tribes. The high councils were largely ineffective, due mostly to the personal animosity shared by the council members, who regarded their fellow members with suspicion. Most of them were loathe to share power with the others. Kirkbride's original job was to serve as adviser to the high council of the regional Arab government of Moab, which was centered in Karak, about 45 miles south of Amman. He arrived in Karak to find the high council willing to turn over its administrative duties to him, mostly because its members knew they could never agree on matters of government, and also because most of them were hardly interested in becoming bureaucrats. And so Kirkbride found himself overwhelmed with such details as scrounging up postage stamps, managing the government's tiny police force of 35 officers, and begging subsidies out of British officials based in Palestine.

Still, there were some moments of excitement in those early years. Soon after he arrived in Jordan, Kirkbride was called on to intervene in a brewing crisis. Abdullah had raised an army of 2,000 troops and intended to march into Syria to expel

The Arab Legion, formed in 1923, maintained order and kept the peace among the tribes in Transjordan. In 1939 John Bagot Glubb, also known as Glubb Pasha, built this police force into the best-trained army in the Arab world. *Above*, King Abdullah I *(second from right)* inspects the mechanized unit of the Arab Legion with Glubb *(center)*, Prince Naif (Abdullah's youngest son, *far right*), and other officers.

the French. Accompanied by the Moab High Council members, Kirkbride rode out to meet with Abdullah, finding the emir preparing his assault at Qatrana, about 25 miles south of Amman. Kirkbride found Abdullah angry about a number of matters—among them the terms of the Balfour Declaration and the establishment of the regional governments, which he felt had usurped his overall authority as emir. Kirkbride charmed the emir, pointing out to Abdullah that the regional governments held no real power, and convincing Abdullah to call off plans to attack Syria. Wrote Kirkbride:

> So the national government of Moab passed away quite painlessly, as did the other autonomous administrations in the north, and the Emir Abdullah set up a central administration in Amman. In due course, the remarkable discovery was made that the clauses of the mandate relating to the national home of the Jews had never been intended to apply to the mandated territory east of the [Jordan] River.

A JEWISH STATE IN THE MIDDLE EAST

In the territory west of the Jordan River, though, developments were occurring in Palestine that would prove to have a profound effect on Jordan for decades to come. Thousands of Jews immigrated to Palestine, many of whom were refugees from Germany and other Nazi-occupied countries. By the end of World War II in 1945, when Adolf Hitler's regime had fallen, the Nazis would have to take responsibility for what has become known as the Holocaust—the genocide of 6 million Jews. The Jews who escaped during the war and immigrated to Palestine were joined after the war by concentration-camp survivors. By 1947, some 600,000 Jews lived in Palestine. That November, the UN officially sanctioned the creation of a Jewish state in Palestine. Under the terms of the UN agreement, Palestine would be subjected to a complicated partitioning in which most of its territory would become the new Jewish state,

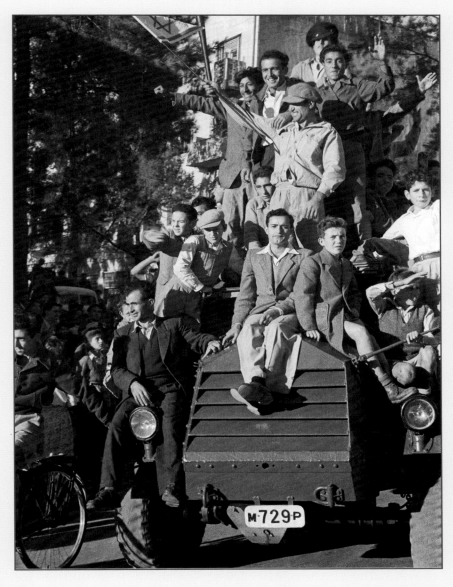

Jewish people continued to consider Israel their spiritual home and the Promised Land, although by the mid-nineteenth century Israel was mostly populated by Muslims and Christian Arabs. On May 14, 1948, David Ben-Gurion and the Jewish provisional government declared Israel's independence. *Above*, Jewish people are celebrating *Yom Ha'atzmaut* (Hebrew: Independence Day). Palestinians call this day *Nakba Day* (Arabic: Catastrophe Day).

known as Israel, while a smaller territory, known as the West Bank, along the Jordan River, would be designated for Arab settlement. The historic city of Jerusalem, site of important Jewish and Muslim shrines, would become an international zone under the authority of the UN.

Jews were not entirely happy with the plan, particularly concerning the status of Jerusalem; nevertheless, they rejoiced. Arabs, however, seethed over the terms, believing them to be far more favorable to the Jews. Indeed, to the Arab citizens of Palestine, it seemed as though their desires were being ignored.

"The Palestinian Arabs had at present no will of their own," suggested Folke Bernadotte, a Swedish diplomat sent to the Middle East to help mediate a settlement. "Neither have they ever developed any specifically Palestinian nationalism. The demand for a separate Arab state in Palestine is consequently relatively weak. It would seem as though in existing circumstances most of the Palestinian Arabs would be quite content to be incorporated in Transjordan."

ABDULLAH IS REWARDED

Meanwhile, during World War II the Arab Legion under Glubb fought alongside the British, helping to deny the Germans a foothold in Iraq, where a pro-Nazi regime was in power. The Arab Legion also participated in a series of battles in Syria and Lebanon against Vichy French troops that were loyal to Hitler. The so-called Syria-Lebanon Campaign helped destroy Vichy French forces in the Middle East.

Following the war, the British—grateful to Abdullah for remaining loyal—finally relinquished their mandate over the Transjordan emirate. On March 26, 1946, Abdullah negotiated a treaty with the British that granted full independence to the country. On May 25, the parliament declared Abdullah king. The country was renamed the Hashemite Kingdom of Jordan.

The Little King

It appeared Abdullah's first duty as king would be to lead his country into war. Violence broke out soon after the UN vote granting statehood to Israel; riots erupted in Palestine, and 62 Jews and 32 Arabs were killed in the first seven days following the vote. Despite Abdullah's high regard for the Jews and desire to live in peace with the residents of a Jewish state, the king found that he could not abandon the Arab citizens across the Jordan River. Further complicating matters was the status of Jerusalem, which was geographically located in the West Bank but which, under the UN vote, remained an international city. Neither the Jews nor the Arabs were satisfied with that "solution."

DECLARATION OF WAR

By the spring of 1948, there appeared to be no hope for a peaceful resolution. Both sides took up arms. One of the first major battles was fought at Deir Yassin, an Arab village that overlooked the highway leading to Jerusalem. Deir Yassin was considered strategically important because a well-armed group of soldiers hidden in the village could ambush convoys and troops heading for Jerusalem. About 100 members of a Jewish guerrilla group known as the Irgun attacked the town on April 9. They were met with armed resistance by villagers. The siege took hours. Some 200 Arabs were killed in the fighting, while the Irgun lost four soldiers. Both sides claimed atrocities were committed during the fighting: Jews declared that Arabs who surrendered hid guns in their robes, then opened fire on their unsuspecting captors, while Arabs said the Irgun targeted civilians during the battle.

Despite efforts by Israel to keep Jordan out of the war—Israeli diplomat Golda Meyerson (later, she would serve as prime minister as Golda Meir) met twice with Abdullah, hoping to keep him from committing his troops. Nevertheless, on May 4, 1948, the Arab Legion attacked the Jewish settlement of Kfar Etzion. After a day of fierce fighting, the Arabs were forced to retreat. They returned a week later and laid siege to the settlement for two days, finally overrunning the badly outnumbered defenders. Many of the Jews were massacred after they surrendered. Kfar Etzion would turn out to be one of the few Jewish losses in the war.

Abdullah announced that he would send the Arab Legion across the Jordan River to Palestine to defend the Arabs living there. Other Arab nations supported Jordan. Egypt, Lebanon, Syria, Saudi Arabia, Yemen, and Iraq joined the coalition as well, forming, with Jordan, the Arab League in 1945.

"[A]ll our efforts to find a peaceful solution to the Palestine problem have failed," declared Abdullah. "The only way left for us is war. I will have the pleasure and honor to save Palestine."

ISRAEL UNDER ATTACK

Israel's Independence Day was set for May 14, 1948, the day the British Mandate officially ended. On May 15, the armies of five Arab nations attacked Israel.

On paper, it appeared the Jews were vastly outnumbered. After all, Israel's population was 600,000; the defenders would be facing armies representing a combined population of some 40 million Arabs. Israeli army chief, Yigael Yadin, told Prime Minister David Ben-Gurion: "The best we can tell you is that we have a 50/50 chance."

Abdullah also harbored concerns. He knew that both the United States and the Soviet Union favored creating a Jewish state and doubted the reliability of some of the British officers in the Arab Legion, but he also knew that all other Arab leaders (including his cousins in Iraq) strongly favored going to war. Abdullah realized that he stood to gain the most land if the Arab armies defeated the Jews, as most observers thought they would.

The Arab League sent some 20,000 soldiers into Israel. The Egyptian, Syrian, Iraqi, and Lebanese armies were poorly trained, their leaders confused, their tactics questionable, and their men lacking the will to fight. Only Abdullah's Arab Legion held its own in the fighting, but it was hampered by the king's orders not to attack Jewish settlements. Abdullah insisted that the Arab

A series of battles were fought following the formation of the new Jewish state. In an effort to keep the Jews and Arabs from fighting, barbed wire was spread over certain streets in Jerusalem, like Zion Square *(above)*.

Legion's job was to defend Palestinian Arabs, so he limited the legion's role to defensive strategies.

During the war, the Israeli forces won key battles against the poorly trained and ill-equipped Egyptians, but Abdullah's Arab Legion fared much better. Four days after the start of the war, the Jordanian troops under the leadership of John Bagot Glubb made their way to the outskirts of the Old City, the walled enclave of holy shrines within Jerusalem. Other Jordanian troops reached Latrun, just west of Jerusalem, which enabled them to control routes to Jerusalem from the Israeli cities of Tel Aviv and Haifa. From its positions, the Arab Legion was able to hold off advancing Jewish soldiers. By early June, when a UN–brokered peace was declared, the battle for Jerusalem stood at a stalemate with the Jordanians in control of the Old City.

CEASE-FIRE

A truce was negotiated by Folke Bernadotte and took effect June 11. To end the war, Bernadotte offered to redraw the lines of the UN partition. However, under Bernadotte's plan, the status of Jerusalem would remain unclear. Neither side accepted the plan, and hostilities resumed on July 10.

Jordan's Arab Legion suffered the brunt of the new Israeli advance. Within two days of the resumption of fighting, Arab Legion troops were routed from a dozen key villages between Jerusalem and Tel Aviv, as well as from Lod Airport, the largest airport in the Middle East. Among the villages captured by the Israelis were the overwhelmingly Arab settlements of Lydda and Ramle; later, Abdullah shouldered considerable blame from other Arab leaders for not protecting the two villages.

A second truce was declared July 18, although neither side adhered to its terms and sporadic fighting continued for nearly another year. Abdullah pushed the other Arab leaders for a permanent cease-fire, but his pleas were regarded with skepticism by his fellow rulers, who believed his real aim was to absorb Palestine into Jordan. In fact, just before the first truce, when the Arab Legion controlled Jerusalem, Abdullah met in Cairo with the Grand Mufti of Jerusalem, Hajj Amin, who made it clear to Abdullah that he did not favor Jordan's expansion plans. While the second truce was in effect, Arab leaders—without Abdullah's participation—created the All-Palestine Government, with its seat in the Egyptian-controlled territory of Gaza along the Mediterranean Sea. Indeed, even while the Egyptians were still at war with the Israelis, they armed Palestinian Arabs and organized attacks on Jordanian troops.

The All-Palestine Government was short-lived. The Israelis, seemingly unstoppable, arrived in Gaza in October and ejected the Egyptians.

By March 1949, four of the five Arab states had agreed to sign a cease-fire with Israel. Only Iraq refused to sign, but, certainly, the Iraqis were in no position to carry on the war themselves. Iraqi troops returned to Baghdad, and the Israeli War of Independence was over. Jordan formally signed the armistice with Israel on April 3.

ARAB COUNTRIES LOSE THE WAR WITH ISRAEL

The war was a devastating loss to the Arabs. They wound up with less territory than they were guaranteed under the UN partition plan of 1948.

Under the terms of the April 3 cease-fire, Jordan retained control of the West Bank, where some 500,000 Palestinian refugees were now living in squalid and overcrowded refugee camps. Another 100,000 refugees crossed the river, finding a haven in Jordan itself. Many of those refugees looked for a scapegoat—someone to blame for the Arabs' defeat in the war and the loss of their homeland to the Jews.

It did not take them long to find the scapegoat they sought in King Abdullah.

LIFE AFTER THE WAR

Jamal al-Gashey was born in a Palestinian refugee camp. In 1948, his family fled from the Galilee region of Israel, and for the next several years they moved from one refugee camp to another. In the camps, refugees lived in tents or huts they built out of scraps of wood and tin. Disease was rampant, water often scarce. The children wore rags, and their shoes were often made from old rubber tires. Meager rations of food were provided by the UN Relief and Works Agency; families often went hungry.

"I was raised on my family's stories about Palestine, the paradise we were driven from, about how the Jews had stolen our land and expelled us from it, how the Arab leaders had betrayed us," al-Gashey said. "When I was growing up, I thought that there was no future for us unless we returned to Palestine, and that if we didn't return, I would spend my whole life as a refugee, deprived of any kind of human rights."

In 1950, King Abdullah annexed the West Bank, where many of the Palestinians said they would welcome his rule. The Jordanian parliament also passed laws extending citizenship to all Palestinian refugees. For Abdullah, these were bold and dangerous moves. By annexing the West Bank, Abdullah took the exact action the other Arab leaders had feared during the 1948 war—that he would take advantage of the war to extend his country's borders. By making Palestinians citizens of Jordan, he increased the population of his country by a third. Moreover, native Jordanians were now a minority in Jordan. Before the war, the population had been evenly split, with about 500,000 Palestinians and 500,000 Jordanians. Now, with the addition of another 600,000 refugees, the Palestinians outnumbered the native Jordanians more than two to one.

(opposite) In opposition to UN Resolution 181, which called for the partition of Palestine into separate Jewish and Arab states, armies from Egypt, Transjordan, Syria, Lebanon, and Iraq, and Palestinian guerrillas declared war on the newly created state of Israel. Although Arab forces expected an easy victory, Israel won the war and increased the land under its control beyond what it had been given in the partition plan. Jordan took control of the West Bank and Egypt controlled the Gaza Strip.

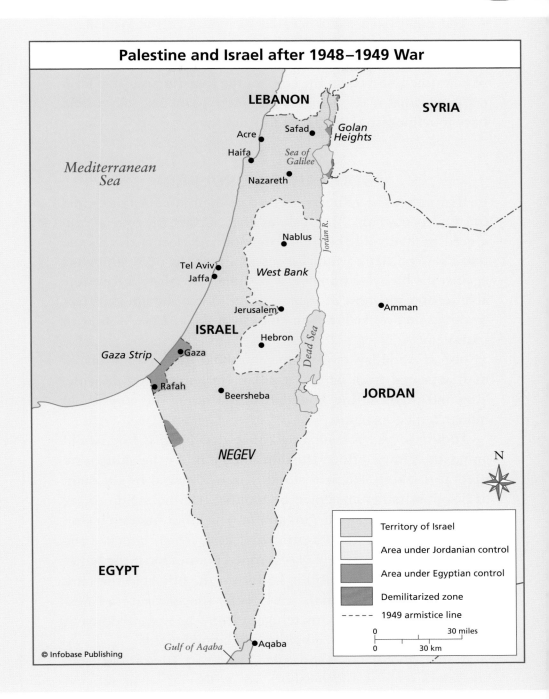

Palestine and Israel after 1948–1949 War

LEBANON

SYRIA

Acre
Safad
Golan Heights

Haifa
Sea of Galilee

Mediterranean Sea

Nazareth

Nablus

Jordan R.

Tel Aviv
Jaffa

West Bank

Jerusalem

Amman

ISRAEL

Hebron

Dead Sea

Gaza Strip
Gaza

Rafah

Beersheba

JORDAN

NEGEV

N

EGYPT

Gulf of Aqaba
Aqaba

© Infobase Publishing

	Territory of Israel
	Area under Jordanian control
	Area under Egyptian control
	Demilitarized zone
- - - - -	1949 armistice line

0   30 miles

0   30 km

The other Arab states refused to recognize the West Bank annexation as well as the Jordanian citizenship of the Palestinians. Arab leaders were still determined to drive the Israelis out of Palestine and reclaim the land for the Palestinians. Arab leaders feared that if the refugees became Jordanians, they would have to relinquish their claims to Palestine.

ABDULLAH IS MURDERED

In the camps, the refugees seethed at their circumstances and quickly focused on Abdullah as the culprit. They were convinced he had sold them out, intentionally losing the war so that the West Bank would be his to annex. By 1951, the plots against his life were numerous. Abdullah's security forces were able to uncover most of them, but on July 20 he ignored their warnings and walked into an ambush at the al-Aqsa Mosque in Jerusalem.

Just as Abdullah crossed the threshold into the mosque, a man appeared from behind a pillar. He pointed a gun at the king and fired, hitting Abdullah in the head. The 69-year-old monarch died instantly.

Abdullah was accompanied that day by his 15-year-old grandson, crown prince Hussein ibn Talal. As the shots were fired at the king, Hussein stood frozen, shocked by the sight of his grandfather cut down by a bullet. He looked up to see the assassin pointing the gun at him. The killer fired off a shot and Hussein felt a thud against his chest, which knocked the prince backward. Hussein was stunned but not hurt; the bullet struck a medal pinned to his uniform—the boy held the rank of captain in the Jordanian army. As for the assassin—a Palestinian living in a West Bank refugee camp—he was cut down in a fusillade of bullets fired by the king's bodyguards.

At first, Abdullah was succeeded by his son, 40-year-old Talal, but Talal's reign would be short. For years, Talal had suffered from schizophrenia, and within months the illness became apparent to government leaders in Amman. The Jordanian parliament was forced to remove Talal from power.

Parliament turned to Talal's son Hussein, who had been Abdullah's favorite grandson. Indeed, the king had elevated Hussein to crown prince just months before his death. Abdullah had seen Hussein grow into a natural leader who inspired confidence and courage in others. "He is the elite of the elite," said Abdullah. "He is the continuity of my dynasty."

During his father's brief reign, Hussein had been sent to school in England. When he returned to Amman he was just 16 years old. Under Jordanian law, Hussein could not take the throne until he turned 18, so for the next two years the government of Jordan was administered by the cabinet, which was composed of men appointed by Abdullah. They were well aware that Hussein had been the old king's favorite and his choice to eventually succeed him. They were thus fiercely loyal to Hussein and protected his life closely. On May 2, 1953, Hussein took the throne as king of Jordan.

To diplomats, he was known as the Little King, a nickname due mostly to his diminutive stature—Hussein stood just five feet four inches tall. But also, the nickname reflected what appeared to be his unwillingness to take his rule seriously. Hussein soon earned a reputation as a playboy who loved parties and the company of beautiful women. Many observers believed Hussein had no interest in the government and would leave the chores of running the country to others.

Meanwhile, in the rest of the Arab world, power was changing hands as well—usually with a large dose of violence. In Syria, two violent coups were staged by army officers in 1949. In Iraq, army officers murdered members of the royal family. In Egypt, opposition to King Farouk's corrupt regime culminated in a coup staged by army officers in 1952. Farouk was exiled and, eventually, a colonel named Gamal Abdel Nasser seized control of the government. Nasser would prove to be a devious and influential player in Middle East affairs for nearly the next 20 years.

And so King Hussein took power during a time of great turbulence—in Jordan as well as in other states of the Middle East. The young king would waste little time placing his signature on the growing tensions.

Pictured is 18-year-old King Hussein *(left)* with Major General John Glubb (Glubb Pasha) *(right)* during a military ceremony at the Arab Legion in April 1953. Rising nationalism among the public led to the resentment of Glubb Pasha and other high-ranking British officials. King Hussein dismissed Glubb in 1956 in an effort to disprove the assertion by Arab nationalists that foreigners held too much influence over Hussein's regime.

To rule Jordan, Hussein knew he would need the unquestioned loyalty of the Arab Legion. Although the legion had fought bravely in 1948, there had been a considerable amount of grumbling in the ranks among Jordanian soldiers since the end of the war about their British leaders, including Glubb and other English officers who held ranking positions in the military.

GLUBB IS DISMISSED

Moreover, Glubb and the other English officers were singled out by Nasser as well as Palestinian leaders as proof that Hussein was under the influence of foreigners. Arab radio broadcasts as well as Arab newspapers aired daily attacks on Glubb.

Hussein decided he had no choice but to dismiss Glubb. The king knew that by sacking Glubb he would risk the wrath of the British government, which was still providing the Arab Legion with $25 million a year in aid. But on March 1, 1956, Glubb was summoned to the office of Prime Minister Samir Rifai, who told him: "His Majesty the King orders that you take a rest."

"Is he annoyed about something?" Glubb responded. "I had a long and very cordial audience with him only yesterday. What is wrong?"

The prime minister declined to answer, asking simply, "Can you leave immediately?"

Glubb asked him what he meant by "immediately."

"Say at 4 o'clock this afternoon," Rifai responded. "We will give you an airplane."

Glubb and his family were hurried to a waiting plane, where they were whisked out of Jordan—quite an ignominious send-off for the man who had built the Arab Legion into the Middle East's best fighting force; nevertheless, Hussein aimed to show his soldiers that the Jordanian army would be under the command of Jordanian officers. As for the British, they quickly ended Jordan's military subsidy.

5

Charting a Dangerous Course

The young king enjoyed adventure. He flew airplanes, skied down dangerous Alpine slopes, fenced with the Arab sword known as the scimitar, and was an avid skydiver. One day he raced his expensive Mercedes-Benz sports car along an airport runway, reaching speeds of 150 miles per hour. "I think she could have done better, but the runway wasn't long enough," he said.

At times, the king seemed fearless. Once, the front wheel of his airplane failed to lock into place as he approached the airport in Amman for a landing. After several nervous minutes, Hussein jolted the landing gear into place by exploding a bottle of compressed air just over the wheel. The plane landed safely. "All this worry about my flying is silly," he told friends on the ground. "I've taken off from the desert at night by the lights of automobile head lamps. I've flown with over-weight loads and in all kinds of weather. Flying is safe enough for anyone with a good head and a good aircraft."

Although Hussein enjoyed playing hard, after sacking Glubb, the king took his role as head of his country's army very seriously. He had no reservations about donning a soldier's uniform, strapping a sidearm to his hip, and traipsing into the field to mingle with the frontline troops of Jordan's army. The soldiers respected Hussein and pledged their loyalty to him, becoming vital allies to Hussein as he found himself pitted against numerous intriguers and assassins who aimed to oust him from the throne.

Indeed, while Hussein scored an important victory among his people by firing Glubb, his next move, elevating Colonel Ali Abu Nuwar to head the Arab Legion, would prove to be a mistake.

Outside Jordan, Nasser and other Arabic leaders attempted to isolate Israel by denying ships bound for Israel the use of the Suez Canal, which links the Red Sea with the Mediterranean Sea. In 1956, Nasser attempted to seize the canal, which was under control of British and French interests. Leaders of the Soviet Union, anxious to extend their influence into the Middle East, made arms available to Egypt. A coordinated response by the Israeli, French, and British armies took back the canal, humiliating Nasser. At that point, U.S. president Dwight D. Eisenhower stepped in and brokered a peace, guaranteeing Israel the right to use the canal. Eisenhower was also alarmed at the Soviet influence in Egypt and regarded Nasser as an unstable dictator. And so he enacted the Eisenhower Doctrine, which guaranteed U.S. aid and military assistance to any Middle East country threatened with Communist aggression.

No longer receiving aid from the British, King Hussein expressed interest in the American offer, contrary to the wishes of many radical members of the Jordanian parliament, who wanted to see the country allied with the Soviets. In 1957, the king's enemies approached Nuwar and convinced him to lead a coup attempt.

Under orders from Nuwar, a division of Jordanian troops mobilized near Amman with orders to capture the king. But senior army officers, fond of the king and suspicious of Nuwar, informed Hussein of the plot. Hussein thwarted the coup attempt by having Nuwar accompany him to an army camp in the town of Zarqa, where he knew he could find loyal troops. The king strode into the ranks of men; the loyal soldiers gathered around Hussein to shake his hand and pledge their allegiance to him. Afterward, the king had Nuwar and the other plotters kicked out of the country.

King Hussein *(left)* replaced Glubb Pasha as head of the Arab Legion with Colonel Ali Abu Nuwar *(right)*. Nuwar's new position allowed him access to the king, and the military officer was soon involved in a plot to overthrow the monarchy. Nuwar remained in exile in Egypt until the king pardoned him, and he eventually returned to Jordan.

There would be other coup attempts. In 1958, Hussein felt confident enough in his regime that year to plan a holiday in Geneva, Switzerland—location of some of the best ski slopes in the world. He sent his family on ahead and planned to join them by flying his own plane to Switzerland. To make the trip, Hussein selected a British-made De Havilland Dove, a small twin-engine passenger plane that was very fast and very maneuverable—exactly the type of plane the king enjoyed flying.

Hussein and his British-trained copilot, Jock Dalgleish, left the airport in Amman the afternoon of November 10, 1958. Dalgleish was a high-ranking officer in the Jordanian air force and a longtime friend of the king. Shortly after Abdullah's murder, Dalgleish had become Hussein's bodyguard, protecting the boy in the frantic first few hours after his grandfather's death. Hussein's uncle, Sharif Nasser bin Jamil, also accompanied the king on the flight. Their intent was to fly first to the island of Cyprus in the eastern Mediterranean to refuel, then head north for Geneva. To reach Cyprus, Hussein needed to fly over Syrian territory.

Later, Hussein would claim that Syrian leaders had been made aware of his plans and granted permission for the flight. Once over Syria, though, the king was advised by the control tower at the airport in Damascus that he did not have clearance and should land at the nearest Syrian airfield. It became obvious to Hussein what the Syrians had in mind: Once the De Havilland Dove landed, he would be taken prisoner.

Suddenly, two Syrian air force jets appeared to the south of the De Havilland. The jets were much faster than Hussein's propeller-driven plane, and within seconds they overtook the De Havilland.

For the next several minutes, Hussein and Dalgleish wrestled with the controls of the De Havilland, working feverishly to escape from the Syrians. Certainly, either of the jets could have shot the unarmed De Havilland down with just a few bursts from its machine guns, but the Syrian pilots seemed to have no interest in shooting down the king's plane. Instead, Hussein realized, the Syrians were trying to force his plane to land or crash into the desert floor—to make it look like an accident. The two jets zoomed past the nose of the tiny plane from opposite directions, each time narrowly missing the De Havilland.

Taking the controls, Dalgleish threw the De Havilland into a power dive and headed straight to the ground. It was a clever but dangerous evasive maneuver. Had the jets followed him down they never would have been able to pull out of their dives before crashing into the desert. But the little De Havilland came out of the power dive nicely. Dalgleish turned the plane south and, flying very low to the ground and beneath Syrian radar, zigzagged his way back to Amman.

Later, Hussein learned that some 200 of his Jordanian opponents had gathered at the airport in Damascus at the invitation of Syrian leaders, who obviously had planned a hostile welcome for a captive Jordanian king.

Following the confrontation with the Syrian jets, there would be other attempts on the king's life—some of them quite bizarre. On August 29, 1960, Hussein was hurrying to a meeting with Hazza al-Majali, his newly appointed prime minister, when two bombs planted in al-Majali's office exploded, killing the prime minister. On another occasion, a chef attempted to poison Hussein's food. Another would-be assassin tried to poison the king's nose drops.

THREATS FROM THE UAR

By 1957, Jordan was desperate for money. The British had cut off their aid the year before, following the firing of John Bagot Glubb. Saddled with responsibility for the Palestinian refugees and with no oil to sell and little farming and industry to generate revenue, the government of Amman had to turn to others for aid. After Hussein's overture to the Americans, the other Arab nations stepped in and offered to make up the subsidy. Saudi Arabia was quick to send money. Syria and Egypt also promised aid, but they stalled on the payments and, instead, started disseminating anti-Hussein propaganda through the Arab print and broadcast media. In June, Jordan ended diplomatic relations with the two states.

On February 1, 1958, Nasser signed a pact with Syrian leaders, agreeing to unite their countries in a federation they called the United Arab Republic (UAR) However, although they were now members of the same federation, Egypt and Syria were not contiguous neighbors. They were separated geographically by Jordan and Israel.

Hussein feared the UAR and signed a mutual aid pact with Iraq, which was ruled by his cousin Faisal. The two countries agreed to face the UAR threat together. Nevertheless, Hussein and his allies in Iraq knew their partnership, which they called the Arab Federation, was no match for the far superior UAR forces.

The Arab Federation lasted just a few months. In July 1958, a military coup in Iraq deposed the royal family, ending the Iraq–Jordan pact. King Hussein—now just 23 years old—found himself standing alone against the UAR threat.

That summer, the British, still fearing Nasser, forgave Hussein for sacking Glubb and sent troops, who took positions on Jordanian soil. Jordan was now a state under protection by the Western powers, who were also allies of Israel. Nasser and other Arab leaders seethed at Hussein's involvement with the West, and vowed to oust the king.

INDUSTRY COMES TO JORDAN

By the early 1960s, with U.S. and British assistance, Jordan slowly started to climb out of the poverty that had plagued the state since its founding. The Jordanians developed cement and phosphate industries and also built a modern oil refinery in their country. No longer a dusty frontier crossroads, Amman was now something of a bustling and busy city, where American-made Buicks and Fords competed for room on the narrow streets with camels and pushcarts. In Amman shops, Jordanians with the means could find American products for sale—Kodak cameras, General Electric appliances, and Palmolive soap. Away from the city, visitors often observed the curious sight of an

American-made automobile parked alongside a tent where a tribal chieftain set up camp.

Hussein also found himself overseeing a construction boom: New homes and hotels were rising quickly out of the Jordanian desert, while the country's cities were being connected by highways that were among the most modern in the Middle East. Tourists were visiting Jordan as well; the country still controlled the Old City in Jerusalem, site of some of the world's oldest religious landmarks.

As for his relations with Nasser and the other hostile Arab leaders, Hussein found them too caught up in their own squabbles to worry much about his country. In 1961, Syria withdrew from the UAR. When Arab leaders met in 1964 in Cairo, Hussein and the other heads of state found Nasser to be far more humble and conciliatory toward them than he had been in the past, as he hoped to build a united front against Israel.

And so King Hussein surveyed all that he had accomplished and declared: "As Jordanians, we have learned one lesson that contributes daily to our progress: we have clarity of purpose. Having escaped death as a nation . . . Jordan wishes to play only one role, that of a model state. . . . We propose to devote . . . our full time and energy to the creation of a way of life that we hope in time all Arabs will achieve."

As it turned out, the king painted too rosy a picture of life in Jordan. Since the end of the 1948 war, the Palestinians remained in the West Bank refugee camps, and their cause seemed as hopeless as ever. For years, the refugees allowed Hussein, Nasser, and the other Arab leaders to argue their cause. Now, it appeared they were ready to take matters into their own hands. They found ways to arm themselves and began plotting terrorist strikes on Israel.

At the 1964 Cairo Conference of Nonaligned Nations, the Arab leaders embraced the idea of a Palestinian uprising and recognized the establishment of the Palestine Liberation Organization (PLO). Hussein agreed to support the PLO, but worried that the group would launch a war against Israel, which would then retaliate against the Arab states. Nobody needed to remind Hussein that Israel had fought two wars against the Arab states and won both of them.

It was also known throughout the Arab world that the PLO included a radical element; various militant groups, including the Popular Front for the Liberation of Palestine and Fatah, from an Arabic word that means "conquest," were operating under the PLO umbrella. Hussein sought to control the PLO leaders and was promised that the organization would take no military action without the consent of the Arab states.

Alas, while Hussein may have believed he had placed effective controls over the PLO, he had no way of controlling Syria and Egypt. The two countries smuggled arms into the Palestinian camps and urged the refugees to make terrorist strikes against Israelis on the other side of the border. In 1965, 35 raids were conducted against Israel. In 1966, Israeli citizens suffered 41 terrorist attacks. During the first four months of 1967, Palestinians launched 37 attacks on Israeli soil. Meanwhile, Israel retaliated. In 1967, Israeli forces raided the West Bank village of al-Samu, contending that the town harbored Palestinian guerrillas. The Israelis razed many homes in the village and arrested residents. When Jordanian troops arrived to repel the invaders, they were ambushed. Eighteen Jordanian soldiers died in the skirmish.

Hussein saw war with Israel brewing and was anxious to avoid a confrontation. He closed PLO headquarters in Jerusalem and had several PLO leaders arrested. But the Egyptians and Syrians continually agitated the radical elements of the PLO, urging them to attack. On May 14, 1967—Independence Day in Israel—Egyptian troops mobilized in the Sinai desert near the Israeli border. Three days later, the Syrian army arrived at the Golan Heights just north of Israel. On May 30, Hussein signed a defense pact with Syria and Egypt, mobilizing the Jordanian army along the Jordan River.

"Our forces are now entirely ready not only to repulse the aggression, but to initiate the act of liberation itself," said Syrian defense minister Hafez al-Assad. "The Syrian army, with its

As other Arab countries encouraged the PLO to rise up against Israel, King Hussein tried to avoid confrontation by having secret meetings with the Israeli government concerning peace and secure borders. In spite of his efforts, the region was soon under siege and an undisclosed number of Jordanians were killed, leading to his signing a military alliance with Egypt and Syria against Israel. Here, a platoon of Israeli Sherman tanks move toward Jordan during the invasion of the West Bank in the Six-Day War, June 6, 1967.

finger on the trigger, is united. . . . I, as a military man, believe that the time has come to enter into a battle of annihilation."

Israel did not wait to see what would happen next. At 7:14 A.M. on June 5, the Israeli air force scrambled and headed for Egypt, where it found all the Egyptian war planes parked on airport tarmacs while their pilots ate breakfast. Within two hours, more than 300 planes—the entire Egyptian air force—had been destroyed. The Israelis also caught the Syrians, Jordanians, and Iraqis asleep, and most of those countries' military aircraft were destroyed as well.

On the second day, Israeli tanks raced across the Sinai desert, met the Egyptian tanks head-on, and soon rolled over them. The Jordanian army attempted an offensive into the West Bank but was driven back across the Jordan River. In the Golan Heights, Syrian troops held their ground until June 9, but Israeli air strikes eventually routed them. By June 10, the war was over. Some 15,000 Egyptians, 2,500 Syrians, and 800 Jordanians died in combat.

The entire war had taken just six days. The Arabs had suffered another humiliating defeat. Now, the Israelis were in control of the Golan Heights, the Gaza Strip, the Sinai desert, the West Bank, and the entire city of Jerusalem. Some 300,000 Palestinians living in the West Bank refugee camps fled across the river to Jordan.

Hussein remembered what had happened to his grandfather when he lost a war to Israel. The king resolved that he would not suffer the same fate.

6

Black September

In the weeks following the Six-Day War, King Hussein became convinced that eviction of the Jews from Israel was not a viable plan. Three times, the armies of the Arab nations battled the Israel Defense Forces and three times the Arabs suffered humiliating defeats. Two decades before, Hussein's grandfather had been willing to recognize the right of Israel to exist. Now, Hussein was ready to make the same concession. Immediately, he called for a conference of Arab leaders so that he could convince them to adopt a similar policy. "We either come out better off now as the result of genuine efforts of all of us to face up to things, or we face some extremely serious possibilities of deterioration in the Arab world," Hussein said. "Even our identity, our ability to maintain ourselves as nations, is involved."

Secretly, Hussein started meeting with Israeli officials.

Jordan lost the most in the war. The West Bank was the location of most of the country's farms; now they were in Israeli hands. Moreover, the country was ill prepared to deal with the new wave of refugees who fled the West Bank and were now forced to live in makeshift camps on the eastern shore of the Jordan River. Once again, Palestinians found the poverty and squalor of the camps unbearable.

Finally, Jordan lost control of eastern Jerusalem, location of the Old City. In 1948, the UN partition plan called for Jerusalem to remain under international jurisdiction and for its sacred shrines to be made accessible to all people. During the 1948 war, the Israelis captured the western half of the city, which contains the residential and business districts, while

As the Six-Day War came to an end, hundreds of thousands of Palestinian refugees poured over the border, crossing the wrecked Allenby Bridge, into Jordan *(above)*. Today, there are 1.7 million registered Palestinian refugees living in Jordan, some still in camps, others in Jordanian towns and small cities. All Palestinian refugees living in Jordan have Jordanian passports.

Abdullah's Arab Legion was able to hold on to and defend Jerusalem's eastern half, which includes the walled Old City. The Israelis moved their parliament, known as the Knesset, to their half of Jerusalem, declaring the city the capital of Israel. In 1950, Abdullah annexed the Old City as well as the remainder of the West Bank territory, making them part of Jordan.

Now, Jerusalem was entirely in the hands of the Israelis. Hussein, as well as other Arab leaders, vowed to win back the Old City and its sacred Muslim shrines.

But Jews and Christians regard Jerusalem as a holy city as well. In biblical times, Jerusalem served as the home of King David and King Solomon, who built many palaces and other ornate buildings in the Old City. Solomon built a great house of worship, known as the Temple of Solomon, and also surrounded the city with a wall. Also, the Western Wall, which the Hebrew king Herod erected 2,000 years ago as part of his temple, remains standing today. Jews throughout the world make pilgrimages to the Western Wall, which they regard as one of their religion's most sacred sites.

According to Christians, Jesus Christ spent his last days on earth in Jerusalem. Also, during the era of the Roman Empire, the Church of the Holy Sepulchre in Jerusalem was built by Emperor Constantine. Other rulers of Rome also erected Christian churches and, indeed, for centuries after the death of Christ the city was dominated by Christians.

In the seventh century, Muslims swept into the city and established their own shrines. It was during this period that the Dome of the Rock was built in Jerusalem. The site is where Muhammad is said to have ascended to heaven.

But the Dome of the Rock symbolizes more than just the birthplace of Islam. It is also a symbol of the conflict that exists between Jews and Muslims, because the Dome of the Rock is believed to be built over the altar of the Temple of Solomon. Following the Six-Day War, the Dome of the Rock was under the control of the Israelis.

Meanwhile, Hussein found his pleas for peace with the Israelis falling on deaf ears. The Soviet Union, anxious to maintain its influence in the Middle East, quickly resupplied Nasser's troops with the tanks, antiaircraft guns, and aircraft lost in the Six-Day War. For three years, Egypt and Israel launched raids against each other's positions. Finally, in August 1970, Henry Kissinger, at the time the national security adviser to U.S. president Richard Nixon, brokered a peace between the two sides.

In 1959, Yasir Arafat, with several former Palestinian refugees from Gaza, founded Fatah, a Palestinian guerrilla group committed to opposing Israel by force. During the late 1960s, Fatah made raids into Israel, mostly from Jordan, causing friction between the Palestinians and the Jordanian government. Later in his career, Arafat, as PLO chairman, engaged in a series of negotiations with Israel to end decades-long conflict.

The Syrians were also loathe to accept the outcome of the Six-Day War. Instead of launching direct attacks on Israel, however, Syrian agents recruited and armed Palestinian terrorists living in Jordan's refugee camps. Soon, a leader of the Palestinians would emerge: Yasir Arafat, a short, plump, unshaven militant who had given up a career as a civil engineer for the Palestinian cause. Born in Egypt to Palestinian parents, Arafat attended Cairo University, where he led demonstrations calling for a Palestinian homeland. Following graduation, he found a job in a cement factory. In 1956, he was called to active duty in the Egyptian army for the Sinai war, but he found himself disagreeing with Nasser's call for a single Arab empire. Palestinians wanted self-rule; they did not want to win back their homeland so they could be ruled by another Arab people. After the war, Arafat found work as an engineer in Kuwait, where he helped found Fatah—at the time a militant organization devoted to armed uprisings.

At first, Arafat had nothing to do with the Palestine Liberation Organization (PLO). The group was founded in 1964 and its first chairman, Ahmed al-Shukairy, was mostly regarded as an uncouth windbag, barely tolerated by the Arab heads of state. Arafat and the other Fatah leaders had no interest in Shukairy's long-winded speeches. In 1965, Fatah boldly announced: "Let the imperialists and Zionists know that the people of Palestine are still in the field of battle and shall never be swept away."

At the time, Arafat was the leader of just 26 poorly armed fighters.

Help would soon arrive. Wealthy Saudi sheiks and other supporters provided money for weapons, while in the refugee camps, Fatah found recruits. These *fedayeen*—an Arabic word that means "people who sacrifice themselves for a cause"—were armed and sent into Israel on terrorist missions.

In 1968, a Fatah bomb exploded under an Israeli school bus, killing an adult and one child and injuring 29 children. The response by the Israel Defense Forces was swift. Israeli agents traced the terrorists responsible for the bombing to the village of Karameh in Jordan. On March 21, Israeli commandos flooded into Karameh; they were met by Fatah guerrillas who fought hard and managed to hold the village. Israeli tank crews soon arrived, but Jordanian army units arrived as well and—against Hussein's orders—engaged the tank crews in battle. By the end of the day, Karameh was leveled, but the Israelis had encountered surprisingly strong resistance and suffered heavy losses. Arafat, who claimed to have taken part in the fighting, declared Karameh a Palestinian victory.

Karameh showed that Fatah could be an effective fighting force. By the end of 1968, some 2,000 recruits from the refugee camps were members of Arafat's Palestinian army. On February 3, 1969, the Palestine Liberation Organization named Arafat its chairman, and Jordan became the base of his operations. From Jordan, the PLO planned and launched its terrorist strikes at Israel.

By 1968, many of those attacks were aimed at planes flown by El Al, Israel's national airline. On July 23, 1968, an El Al plane en route to Israel from Rome was hijacked by Palestinian terrorists. After a forced landing in Algiers, the 42 passengers and crew members were held for five weeks, but they were finally released. On February 18, 1969, terrorists attempted to hijack an El Al plane at the airport in Zurich, Switzerland; a crew member and a terrorist were killed in the exchange of gunfire. On February 10, 1970, an Israeli passenger was killed in an attempted hijacking of an El Al plane in Munich, West Germany.

Israel would strike back hard following such incidents, of which there were many. Hussein found his country constantly pounded by Israeli air strikes.

The PLO was causing Hussein other problems as well. More and more, Arafat seemed to be directing his harshest rhetoric at Hussein, whom he regarded as weak. In October 1968, thousands of fedayeen staged a demonstration and marched through the streets of Amman, shouting anti-Hussein slogans. Clearly, Arafat aimed to demonstrate his power to the king.

Moreover, the fedayeen were hardly proving to be welcome guests. Jordanians knew the Israeli air raids were launched in retaliation to Palestinian terror, and they wished the fedayeen to leave. In addition, many of the fedayeen committed petty crimes, roughing up and robbing Jordanians. Arafat promised Hussein he would rein in his troops, but before long it was clear to Hussein that things were out of control.

On June 7, 1970, American diplomat Morris Draper was kidnapped by terrorists in Amman. He was released after one day of captivity, but three days later another American, U.S. Army major Robert Perry, was murdered by terrorists.

On June 9, the fedayeen attempted to assassinate Hussein. Word had reached Hussein that fedayeen were attacking his intelligence headquarters. Accompanied by two aides and a squadron of soldiers, Hussein drove out to see for himself.

The motorcade was attacked at a crossroads. The king's Land Rover fell under heavy fire, forcing Hussein to jump out of the vehicle and into a roadside ditch. The two aides jumped after him and covered the king with their bodies. The Jordanian soldiers finally drove back the fedayeen assault, allowing Hussein to return to Amman.

"No one—adult or child—could be sure on leaving his house whether his family would see him again. Amman became a virtual battlefield," Hussein said later. "No regular army people could enter the city in uniform, as they would be fired on by the PLO . . . The people in the armed forces began to lose confidence in me."

What to do next? Hussein's more hard-line advisers, including his uncle, army commander Sharif Nasser bin Jamil, and Wasfi al-Tall, a former prime minister, urged Hussein to crack down hard on the fedayeen. Others, including Bahjat Talhouni, the prime minister at the time, urged the king to negotiate with Arafat. Unsure that anything could be accomplished, Hussein reluctantly agreed to talks with the PLO leader.

Hussein and Arafat negotiated a cease-fire, but the fedayeen promptly ignored it. Soon after the pact was signed, 68 people were taken hostage in two Amman hotels. On September 6, Swiss and American airliners were hijacked by terrorists and

In an attempt to force the release of Palestinian prisoners held by Israeli, Swiss, and German governments, the PLO organized several airplane hijackings in September 1970. On September 12, after the release of the hostages and crew on board, three planes were blown up at Dawson's Field in the Jordan desert *(above)*. The hijackings triggered a civil war in Jordan and ultimately King Hussein ejected the PLO from Jordan in 1971.

made to land at a remote Jordanian airstrip. Hussein dispatched troops to the airstrip, where they saw to the release of the passengers. The incident sparked skirmishes elsewhere in Jordan between fedayeen and Hussein's troops.

On September 17, 1970, Syrian tanks crossed over into Jordan to support the fedayeen. Now, the powder keg that Hussein had been sitting atop threatened to explode into an international situation. Hussein asked President Nixon to launch air strikes against the Syrians from the U.S. Navy 6th Fleet anchored in the Mediterranean Sea. Nixon refused, but he suggested that the Israelis may be willing to intervene. Indeed, the Israelis were willing. They considered Hussein a moderate and had been meeting secretly with the king since the Six-Day War. Still, Hussein knew that if he asked the Israelis to defend Jordan, he would be risking the wrath of the other Arab leaders who regarded Israel as their enemy. But there was no question that the Syrians aimed to overthrow Hussein and install a Palestinian-led government in Amman.

By September 19, the fighting was fierce. In the north, the Jordanian army battled the Syrian invaders, while in Amman, fedayeen and Jordanian soldiers fought in the streets. On September 20, Israel mobilized its air and ground forces in preparation, should Hussein authorize the strikes.

Ultimately, Hussein never had to ask for Israel's help. On September 22, the tide suddenly turned in favor of the Jordanian army. Syrian tanks had moved to within 50 miles of Amman, but that's where the advance ended. Jordan hit the Syrians with artillery fire, tanks, and air strikes. The Syrians had foolishly dropped their air cover for the advancing tank force, and the Jordanian jets strafed the tank crews at will. By the end of the day, more than 60 Syrian tanks were reduced to smoldering hulks in the Jordanian desert. Some 600 Syrian soldiers were killed in the battle.

But the fighting in the streets of Amman was still fierce. Such Arab leaders as Nasser in Egypt and Sudan president Gaafar al-Nimeiri pressed Arafat and Hussein to call a truce, but by now Hussein was in no mood to back down. His troops had defeated the Syrians and were now concentrating on the street fighting in Amman. The fedayeen held out until September 25, when Arafat broadcast a message to the fighters over a radio station in Damascus in which he said:

> Our great people, our brave revolutionaries, to avoid more innocent bloodshed, and so that the citizens may care for their wounded and get the necessities of life, I, in my capacity as

supreme commander of the Palestine revolutionary forces, and in response to the appeal by the mission of Arab heads of state, agree to a ceasefire and ask my brothers to observe it provided the other side does the same.

On September 27, Hussein met Arafat in a peace conference in Cairo moderated by Nasser, where the Egyptian leader was able to hammer out something of a cease-fire. Back in Jordan, the fedayeen were still armed and still a formidable military presence. For the next several months, Hussein ruled over an uneasy peace while he quietly rearmed his troops. The Americans and British were now willing to supply Jordan with weapons.

On March 26, 1971, the fedayeen attacked a Jordanian police station in Irbid, Jordan's second-largest city. Hussein unleashed the army with orders to drive the fedayeen from Irbid. On April 6, he ordered the fedayeen out of Amman. By now, greatly outnumbered, the fedayeen left without offering resistance. Elsewhere, the fedayeen were more stubborn. On June 1, a Jordanian farmer was killed by terrorists near the city of Jerash. Hussein ordered Wasfi al-Tall, who had been reappointed prime minister, "to take bold and tough action against the guerrillas."

Al-Tall dispatched the army into the refugee camps with orders to rout the fedayeen. Some 4,000 Palestinians were killed by the soldiers, while thousands more were driven out of Jordan into camps in Lebanon and Syria. By July 1971, the fedayeen threat to Hussein had been eliminated.

An Arafat supporter said later:

We dug our own graves in Jordan. We were welcomed as heroes after Karameh and then driven out like thieves in the night three years later. It did not seem to occur to us that although we shared a common language, culture and religion with the Jordanians, they were in fact in some ways different from us. Some of them had been living in Jordan for centuries and resented our appropriation of their country—or so it must have seemed to them.

The events that led up to the expulsion of the PLO from Jordan became known to Palestinians as Black September to mark the month in 1970 when Hussein put down the uprising. When PLO members resettled in refugee camps in Syria, Lebanon, and other Arab countries, they seethed with hatred for Hussein as well as for their old enemy Israel. Militant leaders in the camps formed a terrorist group with the aim of moving the conflict onto the world stage. They called themselves "Black September" and resolved to strike back at their enemies.

Black September struck first in November 1971, murdering Jordanian prime minister Wasfi al-Tall. An assassin, Ezzat Rabbah, gunned him down outside a hotel in Cairo, Egypt. Egyptian police quickly closed in and apprehended Rabbah and two other conspirators responsible for the murder. As one of the conspirators, Monzer Khalifa, was led away, he shouted: "We are members of Black September!"

Three weeks later, King Hussein's regime was again targeted by Black September. Zaid al-Rifai, Jordan's ambassador to Great Britain, was attacked in downtown London by a terrorist wielding a machine gun.

"I couldn't believe it," said William Parsons, a London electric utility worker who witnessed the attack. "He leveled it at hip height, pulled the trigger, and loosed off about 30 rounds. It was like a scene from a Chicago gangster film."

Miraculously, al-Rifai survived the attack—a bullet sliced through his right hand, but otherwise he was uninjured. Nevertheless, the violence directed toward the prime minister and the ambassador served Black September's purpose—to establish itself as a ruthless terrorist organization, capable of striking quickly against its enemies.

7

Prosperity Amid Turmoil

In September 1970, while King Hussein carried out the defense of his country against Syrian invaders, another event occurred in the Arab world that would have a widespread impact on the Middle East. In Egypt, Gamal Abdel Nasser had been ill for some time, suffering from heart disease and diabetes. On September 28, he died of a heart attack. Nasser had been the Arab world's most vehement enemy of Israel. Nasser's successor was Anwar Sadat, who would prove to be a much different type of leader. He relaxed restrictions on Egyptians, allowing them more personal freedoms. He permitted Egyptian companies to trade with the West. He encouraged tourists to visit the pyramids, the Great Sphinx, and other ancient Egyptian wonders.

And he would take a decidedly different approach toward Israel.

But not immediately. During the Six-Day War, Egypt lost the Sinai desert as well as control of the Suez Canal to Israel. On October 6, 1973, Sadat launched a surprise attack on Israeli positions in the Sinai. The attack occurred on Yom Kippur, the holiest day on the Hebrew calendar. Israelis were caught off guard by the assault and, in the first few days of fighting, were forced to retreat.

Syrian troops participated in the "Yom Kippur War" as well, attacking Israel from the north. During the first two days of the war, some 600,000 Arab troops; 2,000 tanks; and 550 aircraft advanced on the Israeli-held positions.

Jordan did not attack. Sadat and Syrian leader Hafez al-Assad planned the siege on their own. It is doubtful, however, whether Hussein would have participated even if he had known the attack was coming. Although Hussein sent a token brigade of tanks to serve alongside the Syrians, the king had long ago concluded that no matter how overwhelming the odds seemed to be, Israelis always outfought Arabs. He had no intention of sacrificing his main force of soldiers to Israeli defenders. The Israelis were thankful for the king's reluctance to participate in the war; by not having to defend their border against a Jordanian advance, the Israelis were able to send more troops to the Egyptian and Syrian fronts.

At first, the war did not go well for Israel. Using modern weaponry supplied by the Soviet Union, the Egyptians and Syrians outmaneuvered the Israelis and inflicted tremendous damage to their defenses. Nevertheless, Hussein's assessment of Israeli courage under fire proved to be correct. The tide soon turned in favor of the Israelis, who were aided by a massive airlift of American arms.

On October 12, the largest tank battle since World War II erupted in the Sinai desert when 1,000 Israeli and Egyptian tanks clashed. For three days, the two sides bombarded each other from sand dune to sand dune. By late afternoon on October 14, the Egyptians were in retreat. Four days later, Israeli troops were within striking distance of Cairo.

Meanwhile, in the north, Israeli troops pushed the Syrian attackers across the Golan Heights and chased them back to Damascus. On October 12, Israeli soldiers stopped just short of the Syrian capital. It is likely that the Israelis would have invaded the capitals of Syria and Egypt, but the Soviet Union intervened and said it would send troops to stop the Israeli advance. The United States placed its troops on alert as well, which forced the Soviets to back down. On October 22, the Arabs and Israelis accepted the terms of a UN peace resolution: All the territory the Egyptians had seized in the first few days of the war was returned to Israel.

The Jordanians were punished by the other Arab leaders for their refusal to fight in the Yom Kippur War. In 1974, at a summit of Arab leaders in Rabat, Morocco, Jordan was stripped of its responsibility for the Palestinians. The Arab leaders designated the PLO as the sole legitimate representative of the Palestinian people, and ordered Hussein to turn over the West Bank to the Palestinians should the Israelis return it.

This decision would prove to be incredibly shortsighted. As a moderate voice in the Middle East, Hussein was in a far better position to negotiate for the Palestinians than the hard-charging Arafat, who at the time was advocating nothing less than the destruction of the Jewish state. The Israelis respected Hussein and owed him a debt for staying out of the Yom Kippur War. By stripping Hussein of his responsibility for the Palestinians, the other Arab leaders delayed Middle East peace negotiations for years, if not decades.

MORE ECONOMIC GROWTH IN JORDAN

Once the Palestinian threat was removed from Jordan, the country settled in for a period of incredible economic growth. Although oil was never detected beneath Jordanian soil, the Jordanians were able to take advantage of the oil boom. Some 400,000 Jordanians worked in the petroleum industry for the neighboring oil-rich states; many of them sent money home to support their families in Jordan.

Amman became a banking center during the 1970s and 1980s, thanks to the Palestinians who fled Jordan for Syria and who soon found themselves unwelcome guests in that country as well. By 1975, President Assad had forced them to leave Syria; many Palestinians settled in Lebanon, location of many of the Middle East's major banks, causing that country to plunge into a civil war. The city of Beirut became a battle zone. When executives of the banks searched for a stable country where they could reestablish their businesses, they settled on Jordan.

Jordan is one of the most politically open countries in the Middle East. In fact, the 1952 constitution provides for Jordanian citizens to form and join political parties, and King Abdullah II endorses laws supporting the freedom of expression. During the 2007 election season, candidates for parliament initiated intense campaigns *(above)* for votes.

Jordan had always been one of the few states in the Middle East to enjoy a form of democracy. Although the Hashemite sovereign had always been the ultimate authority in the country, a parliament provided people with representation in their government as far back as the 1920s. Following the Six-Day War, though, Hussein found it necessary to suspend parliament, curtail many personal freedoms, and impose martial law due to the threat posed by a potential Israeli invasion and, later, by the Palestinian uprising. Indeed, the last time Jordanians elected members to a parliament had been in 1967—and half of those seats were held by members representing the West Bank, which was now under Israeli occupation.

By 1978, however, Hussein started to ease martial law and return personal freedoms to the Jordanian people. He created the National Consultative Council to temporarily replace the parliament. The council, which was composed of representatives selected by the king, governed the state until 1984, when Hussein decreed that elections could be held for a new parliament. The West Bank elected members to the new parliament, but Israel, fearing they were PLO supporters, prohibited the West Bank members from taking their seats in Amman.

Arafat and other PLO leaders continued to agitate for Palestinian independence. Nevertheless, the PLO blamed Hussein for the woes of the Palestinian people. Palestinians continued to demonstrate against Hussein in the West Bank and even on the streets of Amman. In 1988, police arrested 23 Palestinians in Jordan and charged them with planning to overthrow Hussein's government.

Finally, the king decided to give the West Bank Palestinians the opportunity for self-determination. On July 30, 1988, Hussein announced that he would dissolve parliament, which put an end to West Bank representation in the Jordanian government. The next night, he appeared on national television and announced that he had formally renounced Jordan's claims to the West Bank and East Jerusalem. Hussein said he was ready now to accept the 1974 Rabat decree, which recognized the PLO as the official representative of the Palestinian people. He told Jordanians:

> [T]here is a general Palestinian and Arab orientation which believes in the need to highlight the Palestinian identity in full in all efforts and activities related to the Palestine question and its developments. . . . It has also become clear that there is a general conviction that maintaining the legal and administrative links with the West Bank, and the ensuing Jordanian interaction with our Palestinian brothers under occupation through Jordanian institutions in the occupied territories, contradicts this orientation. It is also viewed that these links hamper the Palestinian struggle to gain international support for the Palestinian cause of a people struggling against foreign occupation.

Now free of the West Bank territory, Hussein did not have to worry about the influence of hard-line West Bank Palestinians elected to the parliament. He gave approval for new elections, and on November 8, 1989, Jordanians elected a parliament.

KING HUSSEIN WEDS LISA HALABY

The 1970s and 1980s also represented an era of change in the king's personal life. His third wife (his first two marriages had ended unhappily), Alia Toukan, was the daughter of a Jordanian diplomat. The couple married in 1972, shortly after the king's second divorce. In 1977, Queen Alia died in a helicopter accident while returning to Amman after visiting a hospital in the southern Jordanian city of Tafila. Hussein was devastated by the loss.

The king spent several months in a deep fit of depression. But during a ceremony to dedicate a new jetliner for Royal Jordanian Airlines, the king was introduced to a young American architect named Lisa Halaby. The tall, strikingly beautiful woman was the granddaughter of the Syrian-born business executive Najeeb Elias Halaby and his Texas-born wife.

They married in 1978. Lisa Halaby converted to Islam and took the name Lisa Noor Al Hussein, which means "Light of Hussein." To the Jordanian people, she was known as Queen Noor, and she would become an immensely popular figure among her husband's subjects. Hussein called her "a Jordanian who belongs to this country with every fiber of her being."

EGYPT SIGNS PEACE TREATY WITH ISRAEL

The Yom Kippur War proved to be a watershed event in the Middle East not only because of its impact on the Arab states but also because of the effect it had on Israelis. Although they won the war, the Israelis suffered great losses in troops and armaments.

In 1977, Israeli prime minister Menachem Begin made an overture of peace to Anwar Sadat: Through secret channels, he offered to return the Sinai desert to the Egyptians if Sadat would sign a treaty guaranteeing peace with Israel. Sadat received the offer warmly. Under a pact negotiated by U.S. president Jimmy Carter known as the Camp David Accords, Egypt agreed to recognize Israel's right to exist. Israel, in turn, agreed to withdraw from the Sinai and provide autonomy to the Palestinians in the West Bank as well as Gaza within five years. On March 26, 1979, Begin and Sadat signed a treaty on the White House lawn.

Other Arab leaders accused Sadat of treason to the Arab cause. Certainly, it was true that Nasser and other Arab leaders had never been able to forge a unified Arab empire and that the Arab heads of state were prone to bickering, treachery, and ambition. Nevertheless, when it came to Israel, the Arab leaders had always spoken with a single voice, and that voice had always called for the destruction of the Jewish state. Now, Sadat had broken ranks and obtained a separate peace. Even King Hussein, believed to be a moderate, criticized Sadat for accepting the peace initiative. "The Egyptians are free to do whatever they think best, although, morally, I feel they should take into

The Camp David Accords with U.S. president Jimmy Carter *(center)*, Egyptian president Anwar Sadat *(left)*, and Israeli prime minister Menachem Begin *(right)* brought forth an unprecedented peace agreement between Egypt and Israel. Egypt regained territory lost in previous wars in this agreement, but angered other Arab governments and groups, who felt betrayed over the peace negotiations.

consideration the interests of the people who've suffered beside them in combat," admonished the king.

Anwar Sadat would pay with his life for making peace with Israel. On October 6, 1981, five Egyptian army soldiers suddenly stepped out of the ranks of a military parade in Cairo and attacked the reviewing stand where Sadat and other leaders of the government were seated. The assassins hurled grenades at the stand and sprayed the dignitaries with machine-gun fire. Twelve people were killed in the attack, including the president of Egypt. The terrorists were quickly captured and eventually executed. Later, the Egyptians learned that the killers had been backed by Libyan dictator Muammar Qaddafi, who was one of the staunchest critics of the Camp David Accords in the Arab world.

Egypt survived the assassination of Sadat. The new president, Hosni Mubarak, remained as committed to the Camp David Accords as his predecessor. Meanwhile, Egypt maintained peace at home.

Other Middle East nations were far less fortunate. In Lebanon, civil war raged from 1975 to 1990, until Syria sent in peacekeepers. The Lebanese conflict affected Americans: In 1983, 241 U.S. troops who had been serving as peacekeepers in the country were killed when a suicide bomber struck their barracks in Beirut.

In 1979, the longtime ruler of Iran, Shah Mohammad Reza Pahlavi, was overthrown during a fundamentalist Islamic revolution led by exiled religious leader Ayatollah Ruhollah Khomeini. The shah had been friendly to the United States, but when he was ousted, Khomeini declared America the enemy of Iran. Islamic militants stormed the U.S. embassy in Tehran and took 52 embassy workers hostage. They were held by the Iranians for 444 days until President Carter was able to negotiate their release.

King Hussein watched the developments in Iran with a growing sense of concern. The shah was a potentate who had ruled over a restless Islamic population while maintaining close ties to the West. Hussein saw himself in a similar situation. To help placate radical Islamic extremists in his own country, he took measures to make the practice of Islam more a part of the day-to-day life in Jordan. The king himself attempted to appear more religiously observant. He also increased state support for mosques and gave Jordanians tax relief if they observed zakat and contributed to charity. Moreover, Hussein ordered nightclubs and bars to close on Islamic holidays and also banned the display of films that Muslim clerics regarded as obscene.

Still, Hussein was concerned with the threat of the Iranian extremists, who vowed to spread their revolution to other Middle East states. And so he enlisted a valuable ally: the Iraqi strongman Saddam Hussein, whose Ba'ath Party came to power in 1968. Saddam had been a leader of the Ba'athists and the true power in the country throughout the 1970s; finally, he ascended to the presidency in 1979.

After a series of border skirmishes, by 1980 Iraq and Iran were engaged in a full-scale war. It has long been suggested by observers that Saddam, later an enemy of the United States, provoked the Iranians into the war at the urging of the United States, which hoped to stem the spread of radical Islam.

Throughout the Iran-Iraq War, Jordan remained a staunch defender of Iraq. King Hussein made several trips to Baghdad to confer with Saddam; the two rulers often held talks while fishing together in the Tigris River. Meanwhile, Jordan and Iraq carried on trade throughout the war. When the Iranian navy blocked Iraq's main port at Basra, Hussein made Jordan's port at Aqaba available to keep the supply chain open to Iraq. And in 1982, King Hussein formed the Yarmuk Brigade, a force of 3,000 Jordanian volunteers who pledged to fight for Iraq. The Iraqis were thankful for Hussein's support, and they regularly turned over to the Jordanian army guns and other military equipment captured from Iranians during the conflict.

The war lasted eight years, ending in a stalemate. The Iran-Iraq War had a devastating impact on Iraq, costing the lives of some 120,000 Iraqis. In addition, to finance the war Saddam had plunged his country into debt—Iraq owed $40 billion to foreign countries that had advanced loans during the fighting. To help rebuild his country, Saddam sought aid from the wealthy oil states, arguing that he had single-handedly stopped

the spread of radical Islam. He found most of them unrespon-
sive to his pleas.

He turned his wrath toward Kuwait, the tiny oil-rich kingdom
that shares a southern border with Iraq. Saddam had long harbored ill feelings toward the Kuwaitis, accusing them of flooding
the market with oil, thus keeping prices low.

When King Hussein refused to send troops for the U.S. campaign to push Iraqi
forces out of Kuwait, suppliers stopped providing oil to Jordan and citizens working
overseas were expelled from foreign countries. In spite of the hardship they were
facing, Jordanians took to the streets in support of their king and the Iraqis *(above)*.

As tensions escalated, King Hussein met separately with Saddam as well as the Kuwaiti rulers in an attempt to mediate the dispute and find a peaceful resolution. Unable to bring the two sides together, the king called President George H. W. Bush on July 31, 1990, and advised him that war seemed inevitable. Two days later, Iraqi troops invaded Kuwait.

An international coalition led by the United States was soon mobilized to oust the Iraqis, but King Hussein elected not to provide troops to the campaign, which would become known as Operation Desert Storm and, later, the Gulf War.

Saddam's army proved to be no match for the coalition; by February 1991, the overmatched Iraqis had been kicked out of Kuwait. Meanwhile, Baghdad and other Iraqi cities took a pounding from a relentless air campaign waged by the United States and other coalition members.

Jordan paid a price for supporting Iraq during the Gulf War. During the conflict, U.S. jets bombed roads in Jordan that led into Iraq, cutting off supplies to Saddam's regime. Many Jordanians died in the bombing runs. Saudi Arabia and Kuwait, which had been selling about 40,000 barrels of oil a day to Jordan, cut off their supplies. Other Arab states also cut off aid to the Hashemite Kingdom. Some 300,000 Jordanians who held jobs in Kuwait and Saudi Arabia were expelled from those countries.

Following the Gulf War, the UN leveled harsh trade restrictions against the Iraqis. Jordan was forced to adhere to the restrictions, even though Iraq was a major trading partner and the kingdom's chief supplier of oil. (Later, the Iraqis were able to resume supplying Jordan with oil.)

Nevertheless, Hussein stood by his support for Iraq and found a tremendous amount of support within Jordan for his position. Jordanians, who had struggled to build their economy without the benefit of oil revenue, regarded the Kuwaitis and Saudis as greedy regimes, unwilling to share their wealth with other Arab peoples. They felt that the Iraqis had stopped the spread of the Iranian revolution, and yet they had been turned down in their hour of need by the oil-rich states that, instead, enlisted the help of the Americans and other outsiders to preserve their kingdoms.

The Gulf War had momentarily shifted the world's attention away from the conflict between the Palestinians and Israelis in the West Bank. Indeed, Israel was finding that its war of occupation in the West Bank was proving to be every bit as bloody as the assaults it had suffered in its four wars against the Arab states.

8

Jordan's Delicate Balancing Act

By the early 1990s, the Israelis had grown weary of the constant terrorist attacks waged against them by Palestinians in the cause of winning a homeland. Starting in 1987, the Palestinian *intifada*—an Arabic word that means "shaking off"—was waged against the Israelis. Palestinian youths attacked Israeli soldiers, often by throwing stones, while others gathered on the streets for mass demonstrations. Later, several Palestinians became martyrs by blowing themselves up in suicide attacks against Israelis.

And so the Israelis agreed to open face-to-face talks with the PLO. In a series of talks starting in 1992 in Oslo, Norway, the Israelis agreed to turn over Gaza as well as the city of Jericho in the West Bank to the Palestinians. More significantly, under the Oslo Accords the PLO recognized the Jewish state's right to exist and Israel, in turn, recognized the PLO as the official representative of the Palestinian people. The Israelis also agreed to give Palestinians control over education, taxation, health, tourism, and welfare in the West Bank, but stopped short of granting the PLO total self-government. It was agreed, though, that the two sides would work together to draft a plan that would eventually lead to West Bank independence. The Israeli army would remain in the West Bank and Gaza to protect the Israeli settlements there. The formal agreement, known as the Declaration of Principles, was signed in Washington, D.C., on the White House lawn on September 13, 1993.

U. S. president Bill Clinton presides over White House ceremonies marking the signing of the peace accord between Jordan and Israel, with Israeli prime minister Yitzhak Rabin *(right)* and Jordan's King Hussein *(left)*, on July 25, 1994.

With peace declared between the PLO and Israel, King Hussein seized the initiative and proposed his own treaty with the Jewish state. On July 25, 1994, Hussein and Israeli prime minister Yitzhak Rabin agreed to the terms of a treaty that would open the borders of the two countries. The treaty stated: "Jordan and Israel aim at the achievement of a just, lasting and comprehensive peace. . . . [T]he long conflict between the two states is now coming to an end. . . . [T]he state of belligerency between Jordan and Israel has been terminated."

The treaty, which was formally signed on October 26, 1994, on a strip of desert known as Wadi Arava along the Israeli-Jordanian border, opened border crossings between the two countries. It connected Israeli and Jordanian utility lines, opened each other's airports to Israeli and Jordanian planes, exchanged ambassadors, and ended a trade boycott the two nations had observed against one another for decades.

"It is not only our two states that are making peace with each other today, not only our nations that are shaking hands in Arava," Rabin said. "You and I, Your Majesty, are making peace here, our own peace: the peace of soldiers and the peace of friends."

The Americans were also delighted with the peace initiative. President Bill Clinton traveled to Amman, where he addressed the Jordanian parliament and announced that he would write off Jordan's American debts, provide military aid, and regard Jordan as an ally of the United States.

Jordan's relations with the Israelis remained cordial, but they were often strained. After Rabin's death, hard-line Israeli leaders expanded Jewish settlements in the West Bank, angering Hussein as well as Arafat, inasmuch as the Oslo Accords required the Israelis and the newly formed Palestinian National Authority to be working toward West Bank autonomy. Meanwhile, Palestinian terrorist groups that Arafat found himself unable to control waged attacks on Israeli citizens. The groups, such as Hamas and Islamic Jihad, made use of suicide bombers to commit terrorism. Israel responded to the attacks with deadly air strikes aimed at terrorist strongholds. By 2002, relations between the Palestinian terrorists and Israelis had degenerated into warfare.

Arafat died in 2004. By then, he had converted his Fatah movement from a terrorist organization into a legitimate political party. At first, Fatah dominated Palestinian elections, but Arafat's death left a void in the movement's leadership. In 2006, a slate of Hamas candidates took control of the Palestinian parliament. A year later, open warfare between the Hamas militia and the legitimate Palestinian National Authority government broke out in Gaza. Hamas was able to take control of Gaza, while in the West Bank, the Fatah-led government of Palestinian National Authority president Mahmoud Abbas struggled to maintain order. Amid such turmoil, Israelis believe independence for the West Bank is virtually unthinkable.

SUCCEEDING HUSSEIN

In 1998, King Hussein started suffering from weight loss, occasional fever, and fatigue. A medical examination uncovered cancer in his lymph glands. In July, the king traveled to the Mayo Clinic in Minnesota to begin chemotherapy. He spent several months in Minnesota, but left the hospital occasionally for diplomatic duties. In October, Hussein made an appearance at the Wye River Plantation near Washington, D.C., where President Clinton had been overseeing talks between Arafat and Israeli prime minister Benjamin Netanyahu. The world leaders meeting at Wye River could not help but notice the king had lost considerable weight and had gone bald from the chemotherapy treatments. Clearly, the king was dying.

In a radio broadcast from the Mayo Clinic sent back to Jordan, Hussein told his people: "My general condition is excellent, my mind is clear, and my morale is high. This is a new battle among the many battles and, with God's help, we will overcome this problem."

Nevertheless, Hussein did not believe that he would survive his ordeal with cancer, and he took steps to secure his throne's succession.

Since 1965, the crown prince of Jordan had been Hussein's brother Hassan. Over the years, Hassan had never endeared himself to the Jordanian people and often angered Hussein by meddling in the affairs of the army. Hassan was also believed to be cold toward the king's wife, Queen Noor. Before leaving for the Mayo Clinic, Hussein spoke with Hassan, questioning his 51-year-old brother on the role Noor and his children would play in the selection of the crown prince following Hassan's

An experienced army man, King Abdullah II was unexpectedly chosen to succeed his father as the next leader of Jordan. While some Jordanians may not have chosen Abdullah as their first choice for king, his decorated military history and Palestinian wife, Queen Rania, made him popular with most of the public. *Above*, Queen Rania and King Abdullah II with their children in 2007.

succession to the throne. Hussein specifically asked that a Hashemite family council be established to advise Hassan on the selection, and that one of the king's sons be selected as crown prince. But Hassan insisted such matters could wait until after the king's passing. On January 19, 1999, Hussein returned to Jordan. He had decided that Hassan would not succeed him to the Hashemite throne.

Instead, he named his oldest son, Abdullah, crown prince. Abdullah, 36, was a career army officer. His mother was Hussein's second wife, an English woman named Toni Gardner whom the king divorced in 1972. Hard-line Jordanians questioned the selection, inasmuch as Abdullah was half English. But as a career soldier, Abdullah knew he could count on the unquestioned loyalty of the Jordanian army. Moreover, Abdullah was married to Princess Rania, a West Bank Palestinian. Therefore, Palestinians, who still made up half of Jordan's population, could find a reason to support the crown prince.

King Hussein spent just a few days in Jordan before returning to the Mayo Clinic. The king received more chemotherapy treatments, then underwent a bone marrow transplant, which failed to alleviate the cancer. On February 5, the king lost consciousness. He was flown home to Jordan. On February 7, 1999, after ruling Jordan for 46 years, Hussein ibn Talal died. He was 63 years old.

The crown prince was declared King Abdullah II two hours after the death of his father.

ABDULLAH RULES

Since assuming power, Abdullah has carried out his father's policies, observing the treaty with Israel, supporting the United States, and continuing to work for peace in the Middle East. In fact, Abdullah has emerged as an influential figure in the stalled peace talks between the Israelis and the Palestinians. He has often acted as a mediator, hoping to use his friendship with both sides to bring them back to the bargaining table. In

2007, Abdullah held a series of meetings with Israeli officials as well as Palestinian leaders in the West Bank. Abdullah told the two sides that unless they act soon, the situation would continue to deteriorate. Clearly, though, the king also realizes that the Israelis will never negotiate with Hamas and that Fatah must take firm control of the Palestinian National Authority before talks about establishing a Palestinian homeland in the West Bank can resume.

The king has also traveled extensively. In 2005, he met with Pope Benedict XVI in Rome, and in 2007, he visited Washington, D.C., and addressed the U.S. Congress. Clearly, Abdullah has used his influence to help spark a dialogue among Jews, Christians, and Muslims. Said Joseph Lumbard, an American who advises Abdullah, "The historic significance is, a Muslim head of state is affirming that we are all part of the same religious tradition, the Judeo-Christian-Islamic tradition."

The king has also worked hard to improve the quality of life for the 6 million citizens of Jordan by introducing a number of democratic reforms. At the same time, though, he has found it necessary to use forceful tactics to maintain control over the growing movement of Islamic extremism in his country. For Abdullah, it has been a delicate balancing act and—in the minds of some observers—not one that he has successfully pulled off.

In 2006, Iranian-born journalist Borzou Daragahi drew many comparisons between the regime of Abdullah and that of Shah Mohammad Reza Pahlavi, the deposed ruler of Iran. Writing in the *Los Angeles Times*, Daragahi pointed out that the shah received substantial military support from the United States and used repressive tactics against his enemies. Many of the experts interviewed by Daragahi speculated that Abdullah may eventually suffer the same fate as the shah. Former U.S. House Foreign Affairs Committee staff member Ivan Eland told Daragahi, "[Abdullah] has gotten more in bed with the United States. He hasn't been distancing himself from American policy. That has put him in a hole he hasn't been able to get out of."

Abdullah's main challenge has been convincing Jordanians that he deserves the throne. Abdullah was educated in Great Britain and the United States. His Arabic is said to be less than impeccable. And he has often found it difficult to free himself from his father's shadow. Nearly a decade after his death, King Hussein remains a beloved figure in Jordan—a factor that may explain Abdullah's decision to strip his half brother, Hamzah, of his title as crown prince.

Hamzah is the son of King Hussein and Queen Noor. Shortly after Abdullah took the throne of Jordan, he named Hamzah crown prince. Hamzah, who was born in 1980, has grown into a mirror image of his father. The physical resemblance is astonishing. One friend of the family told *Newsweek* magazine, "He looks, walks, acts and talks like his father. It's incredible, right down to the hand gestures." Political insiders in Jordan believe that is why Abdullah stripped Hamzah of his title as crown prince; the king fears that in an uprising, the people would look toward Hamzah to lead them. Instead, Abdullah has named his eldest son, Hussein, as the new crown prince.

Meanwhile, though, Abdullah has taken steps to bring reform to Jordan. Soon after taking the throne, Abdullah took the unusual step of disguising himself, then making secret visits to hospitals, government offices, and other public institutions to see for himself how well they served the needs of Jordanians. After making the visits, Abdullah concluded that public services in Jordan could be improved, particularly in the area of health care. Using assistance from the U.S. government, Abdullah renovated and upgraded Jordan's 380 hospitals and clinics, purchased new furnishings and medical equipment, and provided training for health-care professionals. According to the U.S. Agency for International Development (USAID), there has been some improvement in Jordanian health care but medical services in the country can be further upgraded. The agency found that Jordan continues to "have less than fully functional public health systems, a significant demand for high quality maternal-child health care services and information, and a significant increase in the prevalence of chronic diseases."

Nevertheless, the agency also found that Jordan has a very low rate of infection of Acquired Immune Deficiency Syndrome (AIDS), the often-fatal disease that has reached epidemic proportions in many other countries, particularly in Africa. In addition, the agency found that Jordan has one of the lowest infant mortality rates as well as one of the highest rates for life expectancy in the Middle East.

Abdullah has also introduced political reforms. Under the Jordanian constitution, the king is absolute monarch; nevertheless, Jordan's parliament has the power to enact laws. (As king, Abdullah enjoys similar powers as the U.S. president—he must sign legislation in order for it to be enacted, and he also holds veto power over legislation.) Soon after becoming king, Abdullah met with the heads of Jordan's political parties and urged them to participate in local and parliamentary elections. In 1997, several of the country's conservative parties boycotted that year's parliamentary elections—the first since King Hussein signed the peace treaty with Israel in 1994—to protest the pact with the Jewish state. After Abdullah's overture, the conservative parties agreed to participate in elections.

Nevertheless, Jordan is far from being a true democracy. For example, it is against the law in Jordan to criticize the king. Jordanians who speak publicly against the king or publish criticisms of Abdullah face jail sentences. Therefore, freedom of speech and freedom of the press are not guaranteed in Jordan.

Abdullah has also found himself steering Jordan through an economic downturn. As the price of oil rose in 2007 and 2008, Jordan's economy has suffered. Prior to the ouster of Saddam Hussein, the Iraqi leader had been providing Jordan with cheap oil, but that source was cut off after the U.S.-led invasion in 2003. Abdullah's critics suggest that his government is bloated with bureaucrats and corruption, which has caused a strain on the national treasury. Supporters suggest, though, that Jordan has endured worst crises, and that the country will find a way to overcome its economic woes. Jordanian political analyst Samih Mayta told the *Jerusalem Post*, "We survived in the past, and we will survive now."

PROTECTING JORDAN

In forging close ties to the United States, Abdullah has accepted American aid to improve public services in Jordan. He has also accepted military aid. Jordan's air force includes 16 American-made F-16 fighters, which are among the most advanced fighter aircraft in the world. While several other Middle East countries often obtain armaments from the United States, America is always mindful that the weapons can be used against Israel; therefore, the United States always sells airplanes and other weapons to Arab states that are a cut below what it makes available to the Israelis. However, the F-16s put Jordan's air force on an even standing with Israeli air power.

Elsewhere, Jordanian soldiers are armed with American-made M-16 rifles. They are also equipped with trucks and Humvees provided by the U.S. government. From 2001 through 2006, it is estimated that the United States has provided Jordan with nearly $4 billion in aid—much of it in the form of military hardware.

By making that much military aid available to the Jordanians, the United States has expected them to be an ally in the war on terror. Abdullah has responded by assigning Jordanian intelligence agents to investigate terror plots against the United States that are hatched in the Middle East. Also, Jordan is believed to provide so-called "rendition" sites—secret places where the U.S. Central Intelligence Agency holds terror suspects for interrogations that critics suggest include torture. A report issued in 2007 by the human rights group Amnesty International was critical of Jordan's record in treatment of prisoners. The Amnesty International report said:

> Reports persisted that al-Jafr prison in southeast Jordan was being, or had been, used in coordination with U.S. intelligence

Determined to develop and protect Jordan and its people, King Abdullah has developed friendly relations with the United States and Israel. Although these relationships provide security and financial assistance from abroad, terrorism continues to threaten the stability of the country and the Jordanian monarchy. *Above*, Crown Prince Hamzah *(left)*, Prince Ali *(center)*, and King Abdullah II *(right)* salute during a mass funeral for 13 Jordanian soldiers who were killed during a military exercise in July 2000.

agencies for the secret detention of people suspected by U.S. authorities of possessing information about terrorism. . . . The United Nations Special [Inspector] on torture visited Jordan in June 2006 and described al-Jafr prison as a "punishment center, where detainees are routinely beaten, and subjected to corporal punishment, amounting to torture."

Jordanian officials denied the accusations made by the United Nations inspector as well as those made by Amnesty International; nevertheless, in 2006 Abdullah ordered the al-Jafr prison closed and said he would investigate conditions for prisoners. Still, critics believe Abdullah's government has abused the human rights of Jordan's citizens in the interest of maintaining security. "The security forces are improving at the cost of democracy," insisted Hamzeh Mansur, a leader of the Islamic Action Front, a coalition of Islamic political parties in Jordan.

Although the Jordanian government's tactics in dealing with terror threats has been criticized, there is no question that Jordan has much to fear from terrorism. The 2005 Amman hotel bombings provide evidence of Jordan's vulnerability to terrorism. Those bombings were planned and carried out by Iraqis who snuck into the country. Certainly, though, Jordan must be wary of its own citizens as well. Jordanian citizens have been involved in two recent attempted acts of terrorism that garnered international headlines. In May 2007, a group of six men were arrested in Pennsylvania and New Jersey as they planned a bizarre attack on the Fort Dix U.S. Army base in New Jersey. The men planned to obtain weapons, crash through the fort's gate, and shoot as many soldiers as they could before retreating. One of the men arrested in the plot is a Jordanian, Mohamad Ibrahim Shnewer.

Two months later, a car bomb exploded at the entrance of Glasgow International Airport in Scotland. The attack was bungled; the only people injured were the two men in the car when it ignited outside the airport. Meanwhile, two cars that had been packed with explosives and parked in downtown London failed to explode. British authorities soon determined the three bombings were planned by the same terror cell. Authorities in Great Britain made eight arrests—most of the suspects are physicians from Middle East countries. One of the doctors arrested is a Jordanian of Palestinian heritage, Mohammed Jamil Asha.

Jordan, which is located in one of the most volatile corners of the world, has managed to maintain friendly relations with the United States and Israel. Although Jordan is unlike many Arabic countries in that it has no revenue from oil, its people enjoy one of the highest standards of living in the Middle East. And yet, the Jordanians must be wary of their place in the world as Muslim insurgents gain power and make plans to topple the regime of King Abdullah. Whether Jordan can maintain order and friendly diplomatic relations with the West while protecting the human rights of its people is a question that will likely remain unanswered for many years to come.

Chronology

B.C.

3000 Nomadic tribes establish settlements along the Jordan River.

c. 600 Nabataeans carve the city of Petra out of rocky cliffs.

A.D.

c. 610 The Prophet Muhammad begins reciting the beliefs of Islam.

12th century Muslim leader Saladin establishes an Arab empire.

16th century Ottoman Turks rule much of the Middle East.

1916 Great Arab Revolt ousts the Turks from Arab states.

1917 Balfour Declaration commits Great Britain to establishment of a Jewish state in Palestine.

1921 British diplomat Winston Churchill creates the state of Transjordan out of territory taken from Syria; Hashemite ruler Abdullah is named emir.

1935 Hussein ibn Talal, grandson of Abdullah, is born in Amman, Transjordan.

1946 Great Britain grants independence to Transjordan; Abdullah becomes ruler of the Hashemite Kingdom of Jordan.

1947 United Nations (UN) sanctions the creation of a Jewish state in Palestine across the Jordan River.

1948 Israel defeats the Arab armies of Jordan, Iraq, Syria, Lebanon, and Egypt to win independence.

1950 Abdullah annexes the West Bank, making the Palestinian homeland a part of Jordan.

1951 Abdullah is assassinated; his son, Talal, is briefly king but is removed from office due to mental illness.

1953 Crown Prince Hussein turns 18 and is proclaimed king.

1956 Hussein dismisses John Bagot Glubb as head of the Arab Legion, ending British control over the Jordanian military.

1958 Egypt and Syria form the United Arab Republic (UAR), threatening the autonomy of Jordan.

1964 Arab states recognize establishment of the Palestine Liberation Organization (PLO); terrorist attacks begin on Israel.

1967 Jordan, Syria, and Egypt lose territory to Israel as a result of the Six-Day War.

Timeline

1953
Crown Prince Hussein turns 18 and is proclaimed king

1921
British diplomat Winston Churchill creates the state of Transjordan out of territory taken from Syria; Hashemite ruler Abdullah is named emir

1967
Jordan, Syria, and Egypt lose territory to Israel as a result of the Six-Day War

1921

1970

1946
Great Britain grants independence to Transjordan; Abdullah becomes ruler of the Hashemite Kingdom of Jordan

1970–1971
Hussein fights off a Syrian invasion and puts down a Palestinian uprising, then drives Palestinians out of his country; within a year, some 4,000 Palestinians are killed by Jordanian soldiers

1948
Israel defeats the Arab armies of Jordan, Iraq, Syria, Lebanon, and Egypt to win independence

1968 Armed Palestinian fighters battle Israeli troops in the Jordanian village of Karameh.

1969 Yasir Arafat named PLO chairman.

1970–1971 Hussein fights off a Syrian invasion and puts down a Palestinian uprising, then drives Palestinians out of his country; within a year, some 4,000 Palestinians are killed by Jordanian soldiers.

1971 Jordanian prime minister Wasfi al-Tall is assassinated by the Palestinian group Black September.

1972 Black September terrorists murder 11 Israeli athletes at the Munich Olympics.

1973 Egypt and Syria attack Israel in the Yom Kippur War, but the aggressors are driven back.

1974
Arab leaders strip Jordan of its responsibility for the Palestinians, recognizing the PLO as the sole legitimate representative of the Palestinian people

1994
Jordan signs a peace treaty with Israel

1999
King Hussein dies of cancer; his son Crown Prince Abdullah is proclaimed new king of Jordan

1974

2008

1988
Jordan renounces claims to the West Bank

2007
Jordanians implicated in terrorist plots in Great Britain and the United States; Sajida Mubarak Atrous al-Rishawi, an Iraqi woman, is sentenced to death for the Amman hotel bombings

2008
Spiraling cost of oil sends Jordanian economy into a tailspin

1974 Arab leaders strip Jordan of its responsibility for the Palestinians, recognizing the PLO as the sole legitimate representative of the Palestinian people.

1988 Jordan renounces claims to the West Bank.

1994 Jordan signs a peace treaty with Israel.

1999 King Hussein dies of cancer; his son Crown Prince Abdullah is proclaimed new king of Jordan.

2001 Islamic terrorists crash hijacked airliners into the World Trade Center in New York City and the Pentagon, near Washington, D.C., killing some 3,000 people.

2002 U.S. diplomat Laurence Foley murdered by terrorists in Amman.

2003 The U.S.-led invasion of Iraq begins.

2005 Iraqi terrorists detonate bombs in three Amman hotels, killing 57 people.

2007 Jordanians implicated in terrorist plots in Great Britain and the United States; Sajida Mubarak Atrous al-Rishawi, an Iraqi woman, is sentenced to death for the Amman hotel bombings.

2008 Spiraling cost of oil sends Jordanian economy into a tailspin.

Bibliography

"Arabia Decepta: A People Self-Deluded." *Time,* July 14, 1967.

Broder, John H. "Clinton Gives Condolences and a Pledge of Support." *New York Times,* February 8, 1999.

Cambanis, Thanassis, and Rebecca Sinderbrand. "After Attacks, Jordan Faces Its Vulnerability." *Boston Globe,* November 11, 2005.

Cooperman, Alan. "Jordan's King Abdullah Pushes for Moderation." *Washington Post,* September 14, 2005.

"Could the U.S. Do More to Help Troubled Jordan?" *The Jerusalem Post,* March 9, 2008.

Dallas, Roland. *King Hussein: A Life on the Edge.* New York: Fromm International, 1999.

Daragahi, Borzou. "Jordan's King Risks Shah's Fate, Critics Warn." *Los Angeles Times,* October 1, 2006.

Fattah, Hassan M., and Michael Slakman. "3 Hotels Bombed in Jordan; At Least 57 Die." *New York Times,* November 10, 2005.

Field, Michael. *Inside the Arab World.* Cambridge, Mass.: Harvard University Press, 1994.

Finer, Jonathan, and Naseer Mehdawi. "'The Best Day Became the Worst Day'; a Day After a Suicide Attack Shattered His Wedding, the Groom Buries His Father in Ramshackle Cemetery." *Pittsburgh Post-Gazette,* November 11, 2005.

Friedman, Thomas L. "King Hussein, 1935–1999." *New York Times,* February 8, 1999.

———. "Rabin and Arafat Seal Their Accord as Clinton Applauds 'Brave Gamble.'" *New York Times,* September 14, 1993.

Gilbert, Martin. *Winston Churchill Volume IV: 1916–1922.* Boston: Houghton Mifflin, 1975.

Hallaby, Jamal. "Suicide Bombing Attacks Kill 57 in Jordan." *Washington Post,* November 10, 2005.

Hussein of Jordan. "Holy Land, My Country." *National Geographic,* December 1964.

James, Lawrence. *The Golden Warrior: The Life and Legend of Lawrence of Arabia*. New York: Paragon House, 1993.

Jehl, Douglas. "Hussein of Jordan, Voice for Peace, Dies." *New York Times*, February 8, 1999.

———. "Once Derided, Noor Is Likely to Remain a Power at the Palace." *New York Times*, February 8, 1999.

Lawrence, T.E. *Seven Pillars of Wisdom*. New York: Penguin Books, 1962.

Leprince, V. "Conversation with King Hussein." *Oui*, January 1973.

Lunt, James. *Hussein of Jordan*. New York: William Morrow, 1989.

Marden, Luis. "The Other Side of Jordan." *National Geographic*, December 1964.

Miller, Judith. "Cautious King Took Risks in Straddling Two Worlds." *New York Times*, February 8, 1999.

———. *God Has Ninety-Nine Names: Reporting from a Militant Middle East*. New York: Touchstone, 1997.

Nash, Jay Robert. *Terrorism in the 20th Century*. New York: M. Evans and Company, 1998.

"New Crown Prince: 'Extension of Old King.'" Reuters, February 8, 1999.

Orme, William A. Jr. "Abdullah II: A Military Man and Now Jordan's New Ruler." *New York Times*, February 8, 1999.

Reeve, Simon. *One Day in September*. New York: Arcade Publishing, 2000.

Salibi, Kamal. *The Modern History of Jordan*. New York: I.B. Tauris, 1993.

Sontag, Deborah. "Outpouring of Israeli Grief, and Wariness for the Future." *New York Times*, February 8, 1999.

Spinner, Jackie. "The Amman Bomber Who Failed." *Washington Post*, November 14, 2005.

"The Boy King." *Time*, April 2, 1956.

"The Least Unreasonable Arab." *Time*, July 14, 1967.

Yardley, Michael. *T.E. Lawrence: A Biography*. New York: Stein and Day, 1987.

Web sites

The 1948 War of Independence—Jewish Virtual Library
http://www.us-israel.org/jsource/History/1948toc.html.

Amnesty International Report on Jordan
http://thereport.amnesty.org/eng/Regions/Middle-East-and-North-Africa/Jordan.

Embassy of Jordan
http://www.jordanembassyus.org.

Hashemite Kingdom of Jordan
http://www.kinghussein.gov.jo.

History of Jordan
http://www.kingabdullah.jo.

News Hour Interview with King Hussein
http://www.pbs.org/newshour/bb/middle_east/october96/hussein_10-3.html.

Royalty in Jordan
http://www.royalty.nu/MiddleEast/Jordan/Hussein.html.

U.S. Aid in Jordan
http://www.usaidjordan.org/sectors.cfm?inSector=20.

Further Resources

Abdullah of Jordan. *My Memoirs Completed*. Translated by Harold W. Glidden. London: Longman, 1978.

Dallas, Roland. *King Hussein: A Life on the Edge*. New York: Fromm International, 1999.

Field, Michael. *Inside the Arab World*. Cambridge, Mass.: Harvard University Press, 1994.

Gilbert, Martin. *Winston Churchill*. Boston: Houghton Mifflin, 1975.

Hussein of Jordan. *Uneasy Lies the Head*. London: Heinemann, 1962.

James, Lawrence. *The Golden Warrior: The Life and Legend of Lawrence of Arabia*. New York: Paragon House, 1993.

Lawrence, T.E. *Seven Pillars of Wisdom*. New York: Penguin Books, 1962.

Lunt, James. *Hussein of Jordan*. New York: William Morrow, 1989.

Markarian, Zohrab. *King and Country*. London: Hutchinson Benham, 1986.

Miller, Judith. *God Has Ninety-Nine Names: Reporting from a Militant Middle East*. New York: Touchstone, 1997.

Nash, Jay Robert. *Terrorism in the 20th Century*. New York: M. Evans and Company, 1998.

Reeve, Simon. *One Day in September*. New York: Arcade Publishing, 2000.

Ryan, Curtis. *Jordan in Transition: From Hussein to Abdullah*. Boulder, Colo.: Lynne Rienner Publishers, 2002.

Salibi, Kamal. *The Modern History of Jordan*. New York: I.B. Tauris, 1993.

Sparrow, Gerald. *Hussein of Jordan*. London: George G. Harrap and Company, 1960.

Wilson, Mary C. *King Abdullah, Britain and the Making of Jordan*. Cambridge, England: Cambridge University Press, 1987.

Picture Credits

Index

Arabic names prefixed by al- are indexed under the next element (e.g., Jamal al-Gashey is indexed as Gashey, Jamal al-)

About the Contributors

Author **Hal Marcovitz**, a former journalist, has written more than 100 books for young readers. He lives in Chalfont, Pennsylvania, with his wife, Gail, and daughter, Ashley.

Series editor **Arthur Goldschmidt Jr.** is a retired professor of Middle East History at Penn State University. He has a B.A. in economics from Colby College and his M.A. and Ph.D. degrees from Harvard University in history and Middle Eastern Studies. He is the author of *A Concise History of the Middle East*, which has gone through eight editions, and many books, chapters, and articles about Egypt and other Middle Eastern countries. His most recent publication is *A Brief History of Egypt*, published by Facts On File in 2008. He lives in State College, Pennsylvania, with his wife, Louise. They have two grown sons.